Alpine Refuges

The Architecture and Culture
of Mountain Shelters

gestalten

CONTENTS

4	DEFYING THE INHOSPITABLE: FORM, FUNCTION, AND ALPINE SPIRIT	130	BIVAK II NA JEZERIH *Slovenia*
8	BIVOUAC DU DOLENT *Switzerland*	138	BIVAK NA PREHODAVCIH *Slovenia*
16	TEGERNSEER HÜTTE *Germany*	144	REFUGE DES GRANDS MULETS *France*
22	BIVACCO TITTA RONCONI *Italy*	152	GAPPOHYTTA *Norway*
26	BIVACCO GERVASUTTI *Italy*	158	SKÅPET *Norway*
34	BIVAK POD SKUTO *Slovenia*	164	RABOTHYTTA *Norway*
42	BIVACCO CHENTRE BIONAZ *Italy*	172	HOSPICE DU GRAND-SAINT-BERNARD *Switzerland*
46	BIVACCO EDOARDO CAMARDELLA *Italy*	178	JUBILÄUMSGRATHÜTTE *Germany*
52	CABANE DES VIGNETTES *Switzerland*	184	REFUGE DE L'AIGLE *France*
58	REFUGE DES BOUQUETINS *Switzerland*	190	BERGGASTHAUS AESCHER *Switzerland*
68	BIVOUAC DES PÉRIADES *France*	198	HANNIBAL BIVOUAC *Italy*
76	SVARTTINDHYTTA *Norway*	206	LALIDERERSPITZEN-BIWAK *Austria*
82	RIFUGIO PASSO SANTNER *Italy*	214	MONTE ROSA HÜTTE *Switzerland*
92	JIM HABERL HUT *Canada*	220	CAPANNA REGINA MARGHERITA *Italy*
100	KVERKFJÖLL MOUNTAIN HUT *Iceland*	230	RAMOLHAUS *Austria*
106	SEFTON BIVOUAC *New Zealand*	238	STÜDLHÜTTE *Austria*
114	GRASSENBIWAK *Switzerland*	246	REFUGE DE PRESSET *France*
120	CABANE TORTIN *Switzerland*	254	INDEX

DEFYING THE INHOSPITABLE: FORM, FUNCTION, AND ALPINE SPIRIT

High in the mountains, where landscapes are shaped by ice, stone, and time, alpine refuges offer something rare: a deliberate human presence in places otherwise ruled by wilderness. These buildings are generally not outposts of luxury or comfort for their own sake. They are functional, resilient structures that fulfill a specific purpose—offering shelter, guidance, and respite in some of the most remote terrain on Earth. Yet their significance reaches well beyond mere utility. As architectural responses to extreme environments and as cultural markers embedded in mountaineering history and tradition, alpine refuges embody a meaningful connection between mountains and people.

This book explores alpine refuges as both practical shelters and cultural landmarks—spaces that facilitate human activity in difficult terrain while reflecting the ingenuity and values of the communities that build and maintain them. From guiding climbers through storm-prone ridges to supporting multiday ski tours or hikes, refuges play a critical role in making the mountains accessible. They also contribute to a shared alpine culture, built on respect for nature, interdependence among travelers, and a longstanding commitment to protecting fragile environments while making these awe-inspiring landscapes reachable.

Architecturally, these buildings respond directly to the conditions they face. Their forms are shaped by altitude, isolation, and climate: some hug the land, barely distinguishable from the surrounding rock; others stand boldly against the elements, designed to harness solar energy, collect meltwater, or withstand avalanche paths. Their construction often involves both logistical complexity and design innovation. Whether built from stone, wood, or steel in traditional or modern styles, the huts included in this book reflect a spectrum of approaches to some of architecture's most challenging projects.

Culturally, many of these refuges are touchstones within the broader narrative of mountain exploration. They are staging points for legendary routes, symbols of national alpine identities, and places where generations of climbers, hikers, and skiers have paused between

effort and ambition. The majority are operated by national or local alpine clubs, which not only facilitate access but also foster a culture of stewardship, mutual care, and minimal impact.

In compiling this collection, an effort was made to include a global selection of mountain huts—from the Southern Alps of New Zealand to the Canadian Rockies, the northern reaches of the Arctic, and beyond. However, the European Alps, with their dense concentration of historic and active refuges, constitute a significant portion of the book. The Alps offer not only a remarkable diversity of architecture and landscape but also a longstanding culture of refuge-building that has shaped access to the mountains for over a century.

The huts included were chosen for a variety of reasons: some occupy extraordinary or improbable locations, surrounded by dramatic scenery that amplifies their very presence; others are significant for their role in supporting historic routes or alpine crossings; and still others were selected for their architectural character, whether minimalist bivouacs or larger manned shelters. The intention was to represent a diverse range of geographies and building styles, as well as varying levels of accessibility. Some of the refuges featured are challenging to reach and suitable only for experienced mountaineers. Others can be accessed on a day hike, welcoming those seeking solitude or immersion in high landscapes without requiring specialized skills.

This is not a guidebook with detailed route descriptions or booking information. Instead, it serves as an invitation to discover, imagine, and perhaps seek out a refuge that feels within reach. Nearly all of the huts featured can be booked through their respective alpine clubs, which form the backbone of this extraordinary international network. By supporting these clubs, we help maintain access to the mountains while honoring the rich tradition of shared space, self-reliance, and thoughtful presence in some of the most awe-inspiring environments on Earth.

OPPOSITE: More than just shelter, alpine refuges are cultural landmarks in extreme environments, embodying humanity's deep connection to the mountains.

BIVOUAC DU DOLENT

A compact and vibrant pod at the foot of Mont Dolent with beautiful vistas

LOCATION
ORSIÈRES, SWITZERLAND

COORDINATES
45.927245, 7.069016

ALTITUDE
2,667 M (8,750 FT)

ACCESS
4–5 HOURS

ACCESSIBILITY
YEAR-ROUND

TYPE
BIVOUAC

SLEEPS
12 PEOPLE

POINT OF INTEREST
MONT DOLENT (3,823 M / 12,543 FT)

Perched high on the rocky slopes of Mont Dolent, this simple but futuristic capsule bivouac offers a remote stay surrounded by vistas of the ever-impressive Valais peaks. Bivouac du Dolent is a strategic base for climbers tackling Mont Dolent, a peak famed for its position at the intersection of national borders. It stands on the French side of the mountain, close to Chamonix, yet its location makes it accessible from Italy and Switzerland, fostering a unique sense of adventure for those attempting to summit. The surrounding terrain is demanding—steep glaciers, crevassed snowfields, and precipitous ridges dominate the landscape—but the bivouac provides a vital pause atop the sub-peak La Maye (2,642 m/8,668 ft) that towers high above the quaint ski village of La Fouly.

The unmanned hut is open all year round, offering a remote stay in truly sensational surroundings. While it is not directly on the "normal route" up the southern slopes of Mont Dolent, it offers a more pleasant alternative to the Bivouac Cesare Fiorio. In the summer months, alpine climbers seek its simple comforts as they ascend toward Mont Dolent, traversing the Arête Gallet. Although a modestly graded AD+, meaning fairly difficult, it is a long and beautiful route requiring no shortage of commitment above exposure that demands your fullest attention.

Constructed with the simplest of intentions, Bivouac du Dolent exemplifies the principle that form must follow function. Its compact and stilted structure, designed to endure severe alpine weather, provides little in the way of luxury but everything necessary for survival. The metal-clad exterior resists wind and snow, while the interior—a compact wooden space with sleeping platforms and minimal storage—radiates a simple, welcoming warmth. You'll find plenty of blankets, and now an external solar panel, whose small electrical output powers some lights and a kettle—an unusual luxury in such a remote location.

The hut's resilience lies in its design, which somehow manages to stand out beautifully while still looking like it belongs. By minimizing its ecological footprint, the bivouac ensures that the pristine landscape remains unspoiled, allowing visitors to experience the raw majesty of the mountains as they have stood for about 45 million years.

ABOVE: The hut sleeps a surprising number and offers basic amenities, including lights and a kettle courtesy of an external solar panel.

Beyond its immediate practicalities, Bivouac du Dolent is a cultural artifact and convergence point for diverse mountain communities. Built and maintained by local associations, it reflects the alpine traditions of resourcefulness and shared responsibility. Conversations within its compact walls might take place in three or more languages, reflecting the rich tapestry of traditions and perspectives brought by visitors from across Europe and beyond. The hut becomes not just a shelter but a meeting ground for ideas, stories, and shared experiences—just one of the perks of sleeping in an unmanned bivouac.

To spend a night at Bivouac du Dolent is to experience the raw essence of alpine life. It strips away the distractions of modernity, offering instead the stark clarity of high-altitude existence. The beauty of the experience lies not only in the views—though they are breathtaking—but also in the moments of quiet reflection and connection. In this isolated space, surrounded by towering peaks and vast skies, one gains a deeper appreciation for the resilience of both the human spirit and the natural world.

OPPOSITE: The burnt-orange color of the bivouac comes alive at first light as the upper slopes of Mont Dolent are graced with alpenglow.

BIVOUAC DU DOLENT

TEGERNSEER HÜTTE

A traditional wooden refuge anchored among limestone peaks above the forests of Bavaria

LOCATION
KREUTH, GERMANY

COORDINATES
47.632696, 11.678118

ALTITUDE
1,650 M (5,413 FT)

ACCESS
1–2 HOURS

ACCESSIBILITY
MAY–NOVEMBER

TYPE
REFUGE

SLEEPS
30 PEOPLE

POINTS OF INTEREST
**ROSSSTEIN (1,698 M / 5,571 FT)
HOCHPLATTE (1,592 M / 5,223 FT)
SCHÖNBERG (1,620 M / 5,315 FT)**

Balanced with improbable grace on the narrow saddle between Roßstein and Buchstein in the Bavarian Prealps, the Tegernseer Hütte feels more like a secret carved into the mountain than a structure built upon it. At 1,650 m (5,413 ft) above sea level, it rises from the rock itself, a wooden outpost anchored in stone, offering refuge in one of the most dramatic settings in the region.

The journey begins in the forests below, where steep trails twist upward through stands of spruce and beech. In the early morning, the woods are hushed and green, their silence broken only by the rustle of wind in the undergrowth or the sudden call of a blackbird. In spring and summer, the path is flanked with gentians and alpine roses, while in autumn, the hills blaze with the gold of larch and rust of beech. The ascent is both test and transformation, a passage from the soft world of valley life to the raw clarity of the often-overlooked Prealps.

As the trees thin, the terrain grows rugged. The final climb—part trail, part scramble—follows fixed cables and narrow ledges that demand focus and reward it with awe. Then, almost suddenly, the hut appears, embedded in the ridge between two limestone summits. Its silhouette is stark against the sky, a wooden stronghold framed by sheer cliffs and open air. While the peaks surrounding the Tegernseer Hütte won't take you to breathtaking altitudes, they more than make up for it in their demanding terrain and truly unforgettable alpine vistas over much of the German and Austrian Alps.

Built in 1903 by the Munich section of the German Alpine Club, the Tegernseer Hütte was always intended as more than just shelter. It is a threshold between human presence and nature, between exertion and rest. Its weathered wood exterior speaks of alpine resilience, while inside, the warmth of pine walls and the scent of woodsmoke welcome the weary. The dining room hums with the quiet rituals of mountain life: boots drying by the stove, maps unfolded over a Maß of Bavarian beer, and strangers becoming companions over shared adventure.

From the hut's narrow terrace, the view is astonishing. To the north, the hills roll gently down to Lake Tegernsee, its waters catching the light like hammered silver. Southward, the horizon sharpens—Karwendel,

OPPOSITE: Even though it's not among the highest huts, the views over the alpine meadows to the snow-capped Bavarian and Austrian Alps are spectacular.

Wetterstein, and beyond, the jagged crown of the Central Alps. Dawn and dusk transform the landscape into a theatre of light, the rocks glowing gold and pink, the valleys sinking into shadow.

Mountain climbers have long used the hut as a base for the surrounding climbs, particularly the steep faces of the Buchstein, which still bear the hardware of early pioneers. Reaching this summit on this challenging and highly polished climb is no easy feat. Even in winter, when the hut is closed and snows blanket the range, ski tourers trace silent arcs across the ridgelines, drawn by the same elemental pull.

But the true gift of the Tegernseer Hütte lies in its hospitality, tasty homemade food, and warm ambiance rarely experienced at these heights. Once day visitors make their way down, the hut becomes still as the sun arcs slowly arcs down to the horizon. Up here, one feels suspended—not just above the land, but outside of ordinary time. This is not a hut to be passed over in pursuit of higher summits—for here, too, the mountains speak, and the connection they offer is just as profound.

OPPOSITE: The hut is neatly positioned between Roßstein and Buchstein to soak up every moment of the sunset.

BIVACCO TITTA RONCONI

A bright little cabin perched on a high alpine ridge between Italy and Switzerland

LOCATION
LOMBARDY, ITALY

COORDINATES
46.289029, 9.617394

ALTITUDE
3,168 M (10,394 FT)

ACCESS
8 HOURS

ACCESSIBILITY
YEAR-ROUND

TYPE
BIVOUAC

SLEEPS
6 PEOPLE

POINTS OF INTEREST
**CIMA DELLA BONDASCA OCCIDENTALE (3,267 M / 10,719 FT)
PIZZI GEMELLI (3,262 M / 10,702 FT)**

Stowed precariously on the unforgiving jagged edges of the Bregaglia Range, the Bivacco Titta Ronconi rests in defiant solitude at 3,168 m (10,394 ft), clinging to the narrow pass set amongst towering giants. This is no place to stumble upon; it is earned, step by demanding step, through the steep flanks of a granite labyrinth. The hut is inherently self-selecting—only those with the strongest alpine skills, sense of adventure, and head for heights will make it to Bivacco Titta Ronconi, and therein lies its beauty. The distinctive yellow-and-red metal box stands boldly against the gray teeth of the range, a sudden, jarring blaze of color in a world sculpted by wind, silence, and glaciers.

The Bregaglia Range, straddling the divide between Italy's Val Masino and Switzerland's Val Bregaglia, is one of the Alps' most jagged expressions—an arena of serrated ridgelines, shattered spires, and soaring granite faces. Below, deep, resinous forests thick with larch and spruce sigh in the morning mist. Higher up, the trees yield to tundra and then to bare rock, striated by centuries of glacial activity. Solitude reigns at this altitude, broken only by the sure-footed passage of ibex and chamois, and the sharp whistle of marmots echoing across the wind-scoured scree.

The bivouac itself is modest—a bright, riveted metal shelter bolted directly into the mountain's bones. It sleeps six in close quarters, lined with wooden bunks and alpine austerity. There is no stove, no water, no indulgence. However, it provides something rarer: safety, perspective, and a place to watch the sky slowly catch fire over the granite spires of the Sciora group. On a clear night, the stars seem closer, but bad weather can linger in these high peaks, making the hut an even more valuable lifeline.

Named after Titta Ronconi, a Milanese mountaineer and Italian Alpine Club (CAI) stalwart who dedicated his life to the mountain community, the bivouac is a quiet tribute that honors not grand gestures, but quiet persistence and a reverence for the wildest of places. Installed by the CAI of Milan, it supports climbers and alpinists aiming for the high ridges of the Bondasca basin, facilitating strategic access to the formidable north ridge of Pizzi Gemelli and the sweeping traverses toward Pizzo Badile and Cengalo.

While its elevation and remoteness keep it away from casual visitors, the Bivacco Titta Ronconi is vital for

those pursuing the high, less-traveled lines of the Alps. It marks a threshold where human effort meets the indifferent vastness of the mountain range. The approach from the Italian side, usually beginning in the leafy embrace of Val Porcellizzo, involves a long and rugged ascent, crossing moraines, scrambling through couloirs, and navigating snowy ridgelines where every step must be deliberately confident.

Those who arrive find more than just shelter. They find themselves encircled by granite towers carved in primeval drama, wrapped in a silence so profound, it humbles the heartbeat. To sit at the threshold of Bivacco Titta Ronconi, looking down over the toothy skyline of the Bregaglia, is to understand something enduring: that in places stripped of excess, the essentials grow clearer. After the long and arduous ascent, the stillness here feels earned, where the wind speaks in whispers and only the mountains bear silent witness.

OPPOSITE: Clouds roll over the granite spires of the Adamello-Presanella range. **ABOVE:** This tiny hut features impressive sleeping platforms for six and a fold-away table.

BIVACCO GERVASUTTI

A futuristic modern capsule perched on the edge of the void under the ever-impressive Grandes Jorasses

LOCATION
VAL FERRET, ITALY

COORDINATES
45.875943, 7.013132

ALTITUDE
2,835 M (9,301 FT)

ACCESS
4–6 HOURS

ACCESSIBILITY
YEAR-ROUND

TYPE
BIVOUAC

SLEEPS
12 PEOPLE

POINTS OF INTEREST
**FRÉBOUGE GLACIER
AIGUILLE DE LESCHAUX (3,759 M / 12,333 FT)
GRANDES JORASSES (4,208 M / 13,806 FT)**

Standing on a rocky outcrop at 2,835 m (9,301 ft) above sea level, the Bivacco Gervasutti defies both gravity and expectation. A sleek, tubular capsule clinging to the jagged ridgeline at the foot of the east face of the Grandes Jorasses, it is a striking anomaly in the high alpine landscape—a vision of the future in a land ruled by vast glaciers and towering granite spires. Here, where the Mont Blanc massif unfurls its cathedral towers and the wind carves stories into the snow, the bivouac stands sentinel, offering refuge to those who dare to move within this steep and wild terrain.

The Bivacco Gervasutti is unlike any other mountain shelter. Installed in 2011 as a replacement for the aging wooden structure that had served for decades, it is a marvel of modern engineering. Designed by an Italian engineering firm, the hut is a prefabricated module, airlifted in sections and seamlessly assembled on-site. Its aerodynamic, red-and-white fuselage is both a practical necessity—withstanding the brutal alpine winds—and a bold aesthetic statement. Inside, the space is compact but meticulously designed: a snug wooden interior with bunks for 12, solar-powered lighting, and a digital interface providing weather updates. The hut is dominated by endless panoramic views through the large front window that looks out over Aosta's numerous peaks.

Reaching the Bivacco Gervasutti is a relatively strenuous ascent from Val Ferret, beginning in lush forests before transitioning into steep, rocky hiking and the exposed Borelli Couloir, where careful route-finding is essential. It can also be accessed in the winter months, affording adventurous ski tourers the opportunity to avoid challenging river crossings and technical scrambling, as well as a much higher chance of having the hut to yourself.

Named after Giusto Gervasutti, the legendary Italian alpinist who left his mark on many of the Alps' most formidable faces, the bivouac is more than a shelter—it is an homage to those who push the boundaries of human endurance. Gervasutti himself perished in an avalanche on Mont Blanc du Tacul in 1946, but his spirit endures in the climbers who bunk here, as they prepare for their next challenge.

The hut's location makes it a valuable launching point for some of the most demanding climbs in the

ABOVE: The interior of Bivacco Gervasutti is light and modern, thanks to a large window that perfectly frames Aosta's adjacent peaks like a futuristic painting.

range. Looking higher up the valley, the skyline is dominated by the daunting east face of the Grandes Jorasses, with its labyrinthine seracs and sheer granite walls. In winter, ski tourers chart their own audacious lines through the Frébouge Glacier, weaving through soaring seracs that dwarf passersby.

Yet, for all its high-tech sophistication, the Bivacco Gervasutti remains true to the ethos of a mountain refuge. It is unmanned, free to use, and entirely dependent on the respect of those who visit. The unwritten code of the Alps—leave it as you found it, share it without question—governs life here. A battered guestbook bears witness to camaraderie and solitude alike: exhausted climbers huddling together against the cold, sunrise spilling gold across the glaciers, and the silence of these high places.

The Bivacco Gervasutti is a paradox: an advanced feat of design and an echo of a timeless alpine tradition. It is a place where past and future converge, where the weight of history meets the call of new challenges. And for those who pass through its narrow door, it offers comfort in the heart of the wild.

OPPOSITE: A night in the Gervasutti feels distinctly wild, with only Rifugio Bonatti occasionally shining back. **ABOVE LEFT:** Sunrise graces the iconic Grandes Jorasses.

BIVACCO GERVASUTTI

BIVAK POD SKUTO

A small, contemporary bivouac perched high among the towering peaks of Slovenia's Kamnik-Savinja Alps

LOCATION
KAMNIK-SAVINJA ALPS, SLOVENIA

COORDINATES
46.358998, 14.567881

ALTITUDE
2,070 M (6,791 FT)

ACCESS
4–6 HOURS

ACCESSIBILITY
YEAR-ROUND

TYPE
BIVOUAC

SLEEPS
6–8 PEOPLE

POINTS OF INTEREST
**GRINTOVEC (2,558 M / 8,392 FT)
SKUTA (2,532 M / 8,307 FT)**

Bivak Pod Skuto is a beautifully modern mountain shelter nestled high in the Kamnik-Savinja Alps of Slovenia, offering a refuge for hikers and mountaineers in one of Europe's most stunning mountain ranges. Located at 2,070 m (6,791 ft), the hut grants access to some of the most rugged hiking peaks in the Alps, including Mount Skuta and the Grintovec massif. The Bivak Pod Skuto shelter sleeps around eight guests in basic but cozy conditions, with a simple, functional design that reflects its purpose: to provide shelter and a place to rest for hikers and climbers alike. The hut offers a unique contrast of modern design in wild and rugged terrain, with endless sunset views down the valley.

Initially constructed in 1959, Bivak Pod Skuto's design was simple, reflecting the need for practicality in harsh weather conditions, and incorporating durable materials to withstand the exposed alpine environment. In the early 2000s, the hut was entirely replaced to accommodate the growing number of mountaineers and hikers. The all-new iteration was redesigned in a collaboration between OFIS Architects and students at Harvard Graduate School of Design. The shelter resembles a series of mountain peaks, with its roofline shedding snow and framing distant views. The building's gray, glass-reinforced concrete cladding blends with the surrounding stone, while sustainable features such as natural ventilation, strong insulation, and a lack of electricity preserve its minimalist character. The warm wooden interior of the hut is a welcoming contrast to its somewhat cold exterior.

Bivak Pod Skuto is ideally situated for hikers wishing to explore the abundant peaks in the Kamnik-Savinja Alps or for hiking hut-to-hut through the region. Among those drawn to this rugged corner of Slovenia is mountaineer and outdoor enthusiast Jess Clark, who shares her thoughts on her approach to the hut: "Taking those final footsteps to the top, all our hard work is soon forgotten as the views reveal mountains as far as the eye can see. The pale limestone peaks emerge proudly out of the forests, at times giving the appearance of snowcapped mountains even in summer. At over 2,500 m (8,202 ft) the air is refreshingly cool, contrasting with the gentle warmth of the morning sun, which is now starting to heat up. We pause and take it all in, independently enjoying these special moments of

OPPOSITE: Descending the Skuta peak ridge after a sunrise raid. ABOVE: The wooden interior is compact and minimalist with lots of natural light.

solitude, while also sharing the experience without a single word spoken. The descent is involving and demands our fullest attention, but eventually, this majestic bivouac is in our sights. It's perched neatly on a cliff, which looks out to the forested valley below. Chucking our bags down, we cozy up in the wooden interior, which feels like total luxury despite the minimalist facilities. It's absolutely all we need and so much more."

Reaching the hut is relatively nontechnical, albeit a somewhat strenuous hike. Much of the hiking in the peaks above, however, is not for the faint of heart, with plenty of exposed and technical terrain in many places secured with metal handrails. Bivak Pod Skuto serves as a practical refuge for mountaineers, reflecting Slovenian alpine traditions of self-reliance and simplicity. Its remote location offers a quiet, unobtrusive space to rest, while its surroundings provide an opportunity for reflection and a deeper connection to the harsh-yet-beautiful mountain landscape.

OPPOSITE: A clear night at Bivak Pavla Kemperla, one of the many other bivouacs neatly linked in this part of the Julian Alps.

BIVAK POD SKUTO

BIVACCO CHENTRE BIONAZ

A traditional and charming wooden bivouac in the upper reaches of the remote Valpelline Valley

LOCATION
AOSTA VALLEY, ITALY

COORDINATES
45.880953, 7.479403

ALTITUDE
2,530 M (8,300 FT)

ACCESS
5 HOURS

ACCESSIBILITY
YEAR-ROUND

TYPE
BIVOUAC

SLEEPS
16 PEOPLE

POINT OF INTEREST
BECCA DI LUSENEY (3,502 M / 11,490 FT)

Nestled in the serene embrace of the Italian Alps in the Aosta Valley region, Valpelline is a beautifully wild area where rich forests give way to the tall, rugged alpine spires. Watching over this forgotten valley is the Bivacco Chentre Bionaz—a classic wooden alpine hut that transports you to a simpler time. From here, you can enjoy sprawling vistas of the surrounding peaks while watching the sunset's orange-and-pink hues illuminate the landscape.

Valpelline offers a tranquil escape from the bustling tourist trails. Village life in the area is largely born out of farming and the creation of Fontina cheese from the endless alpine pastures. The small village of Bionaz has retained its traditional character, only getting rudimentary road access as late as 1953.

From the village, the trail winds through dense forests, past cascading waterfalls and across rugged terrain, offering a taste of the natural beauty that defines the region. The hike-or-ski tour is moderately challenging, requiring a good level of fitness and experience in mountain navigation. As the route leaves the forest, the towering peaks become visible, and the hut sits atop a rocky buttress, watching over the meandering valley below.

From the moment Bivacco Chentre Bionaz comes into view, it is evident that this is no ordinary mountain refuge. Its architecture is a fusion of traditional alpine aesthetics, with a dark wooden facade and relatively modern design within. Constructed primarily from metal, the bivouac exudes a rugged charm topped by a uniquely curved roof designed to rid itself of heavy snowfall. Its weathered exterior blends seamlessly with its rocky landscape. The interior offers a surprising number of beds lining the back wall, with additional sleeping on a mezzanine, while still keeping an airy feel. There are two dining and sitting areas and a collection of unique ornaments, including a line of seven sculptured heads lining the walls, which add a distinctive, if slightly enigmatic touch. The shelter is surrounded by towering pinnacles at all angles, offering sweeping views that stretch along the meandering Valpelline valley.

The bivouac is an integral part of the region's rich mountaineering history. In 2010, it was dedicated to Carlo Chentre, mayor of the nearby Bionaz village

OPPOSITE: Morning light washing over the mountain vistas of Valpelline, a lesser-traveled area within the Aosta Valley, especially during the winter months.

from 1974 to 1990 and president of the local ski club, and to Ettore Bionaz, a mountain guide and pioneer of mountain rescue in Valpelline. Bionaz also served as mayor for some years before dying tragically on July 24, 1985, on the Mont Cerf Glacier. Indeed, the *bivacco* feels like a high-altitude outpost for the village and its people.

The area is dominated by the imposing Becca di Luseney (3,502 m/11,490 ft), a classically pyramidal peak with hanging glaciers. In summer, the summit can be reached from the adjacent southeast face. During the winter, very experienced ski mountaineers can climb the steep north-face route, which meanders through numerous rock bands and glaciated terrain. Bivacco Chentre Bionaz not only provides an essential haven for alpinists but also an opportunity for altitude acclimatization along the route.

In the quiet solitude of Bivacco Chentre Bionaz, time seems to stand still, offering a rare communion with nature's raw, unfiltered beauty. This humble refuge is full of rustic character, fostering unforgettable adventures for hikers and skiers all year round.

BIVACCO EDOARDO CAMARDELLA

A beautiful modern high-altitude bivouac with incredible panoramic views of the Mont Blanc massif

LOCATION
AOSTA VALLEY, ITALY

COORDINATES
45.634166, 7.019500

ALTITUDE
3,357 M (11,014 FT)

ACCESS
7 HOURS

ACCESSIBILITY
YEAR-ROUND

TYPE
BIVOUAC

SLEEPS
6 PEOPLE

POINT OF INTEREST
RUTOR GLACIER

Most traditional bivouacs are built to facilitate mountaineering endeavors, offering an essential space for respite toward an otherwise bigger goal. For many, however, Bivacco Edoardo Camardella is both the journey *and* the destination. Standing afoot snowcapped rocky ridges, the hut is surrounded by the sprawling Rutor Glacier and panoramic views of Mont Blanc, Grandes Jorasses, and many other alpine giants. The hut grants a truly unique sense of space and freedom, a sanctuary where the hustle and bustle of everyday life couldn't feel further away. The region was a favorite of La Thuile skier and instructor Edoardo Camardella, who died tragically in an avalanche in 2019.

"Edo" was deeply passionate about skiing big lines and sharing the mountains he called home. Renowned for bringing people together, this bivouac couldn't be more in keeping with his approach to life and legacy. While most refuges are built and owned by traditional alpine clubs, this hut was built entirely in Edo's memory through a vast collaboration between the entire La Thuile community. The hut stands as a beacon for Edo's life-philosophy, as captured beautifully by close friend Federico Gregotti Zoja's poetry:

> Edo's house is already there
> between the earth and the sky,
> between the clouds and the glaciers,
> between the night and the sun.
> The bivouac will have its strong and generous arms,
> ready to welcome those seeking refreshment;
> will have his sincere and smiling eyes
> that will give to every mountaineer
> the warmth you reserve for an old friend.
> There will be room for everyone in Edo's house,
> because it's not just a mountain bivouac
> —immersed in the infinite silence of the snows—
> but a place of the soul and memory.

Reaching Edo's house, however, is no easy feat. In summer, the shortest mountaineering route departs from the village of Valgrisenche—a steep and relentless four- to-five-hour climb. In winter or spring, the hut is reachable by ski-touring from Mont Valaisan, which can be accessed via the La Thuile-La Rosière lift system. Although relatively straightforward, the route is long and will take a full day.

The hut perches on a rocky ridge at the very top of the mellow but seemingly unending Rutor Glacier, one

OPPOSITE: Decals of local businesses and organizations that supported the construction of Bivacco Edoardo Camardella adorn the southeast wall.

of Italy's largest. Angular and modern, the structure's dark aluminum-clad exterior reflects the shifting hues of alpine light, blending harmoniously with its rugged surroundings. The windows overlook the entirety of the Mont Blanc massif and its surrounding peaks. Its asymmetrical silhouette evokes the jagged peaks that frame it, while the muted palette of gray and silver mirrors the rocky terrain.

The light-wooden interior of Bivacco Edoardo Camardella is a study in functionality and warmth. Built to accommodate up to six people, its compact space is carefully optimized for the needs of mountaineers and hikers. Wooden paneling and efficient insulation create a welcoming environment, warding off the biting alpine winds that sweep across the ridges. The bunk beds, lined with simple mattresses and blankets, offer a respite for weary adventurers. A central table invites communal moments, where stories of summits conquered and challenges overcome are shared over modest meals. The large window, strategically placed, frames a breathtaking panorama: a theater of peaks and valleys that shift with the changing seasons.

CABANE DES VIGNETTES

A large traditional stone refuge serving as a crucial waypoint on the legendary Haute Route

LOCATION
AROLLA, SWITZERLAND

COORDINATES
45.989806, 7.475636

ALTITUDE
3,160 M (10,367 FT)

ACCESS
4 HOURS

ACCESSIBILITY
MARCH–MAY & JUNE–SEPTEMBER

TYPE
REFUGE

SLEEPS
120 PEOPLE

POINTS OF INTEREST
PIGNE D'AROLLA (3,787 M / 12,425 FT)
HAUTE ROUTE

Precariously perched high above the icy expanse of the Otemma Glacier, Cabane des Vignettes clings to a rocky promontory at 3,160 m (10,367 ft), a sentinel in the vast, untamed heart of the Pennine Alps. Here, amid a world of ice and stone, the refuge stands as both a lifeline and a landmark, its angular form echoing the jagged peaks surrounding it. Snow-covered summits rise in every direction—the majestic Mont Collon to the north, the distant Dent Blanche piercing the horizon—while an ocean of glaciers flows through the valley and nearby plateaus below.

For many, Cabane des Vignettes marks a pivotal stop on the famed Haute Route, the iconic multiday ski tour from Chamonix to Zermatt. Arriving at the hut can feel like a triumph—a blend of exhaustion and exhilaration as mountaineers settle in for a well-earned rest. Among those drawn to these peaks is professional skier Loïc Isliker, who recalls an unforgettable morning spent at the hut before skiing the iconic north face of Pigne d'Arolla:

"We arrived at Cabane des Vignettes after a long day in the mountains, tired yet excited. The hut's perch above the glacier is unreal; watching the sunset over Mont Collon from the terrace is something I'll never forget. After an early night, we set out before dawn. Standing on the summit of Pigne d'Arolla at 7:00 a.m., the mountains stretched endlessly before us, bathed in golden morning light. The descent down the north face felt surreal—smooth turns through perfect snow, each one a reminder of how fleeting these moments are. Even now, it stands out as one of the greatest ski experiences of my life."

Cabane des Vignettes is a masterpiece of traditional alpine architecture, first brought to life in 1924 by American alpinist Stuart Jenkins. Rebuilt in 1946, the sturdy stone structure remains steeped in alpine character despite now being equipped with modern provisions under the management of the Swiss Alpine Club. The hut's pitched roof sheds the heavy snow that blankets the mountains each winter, and inside, wooden bunks and a communal dining space create a warm, welcoming retreat.

Reaching the hut is no small feat. In summer, the ascent from the village of Arolla is demanding, winding through steep moraine and glacier terrain, with crampons often required for the final icy push. In winter and spring, ski tourers navigate vast, crevassed glaciers, their route dictated by shifting mountain conditions. For those

OPPOSITE: An unusual perch for a refuge of this size, the Cabane des Vignettes stands watchful over the couloir below that shares its name.

seeking a challenge, the hut can be reached in a single-day tour from Cabane de Bertol or Cabane des Dix, or for the wildly ambitious, the daring 30-kilometer (18.6-mile) ski descent to Zermatt offers an unforgettable finale.

For all its charm, Cabane des Vignettes reminds us of the alpine wilderness's unpredictable nature. In 2018, a tragic storm claimed the lives of seven ski tourers—just 550 m (1,804 ft) from the hut—when rapidly worsening conditions turned their route into a deadly trap. Known as "Le Drame des Alpes valaisannes", this incident remains a stark reminder of how unforgiving these mountains can be.

Yet, despite the challenges, moments of connection abound. In spring, the hut's terrace hums with life—skiers basking in the sun, recounting their routes and sharing quiet moments of reflection. Suspended above the glacier, Cabane des Vignettes feels like an outpost at the world's edge—remote yet profoundly human. It is a beacon of resilience and camaraderie, a reminder that even the simplest refuge can feel like home in the vastness of the high mountains.

OPPOSITE: Two ski tourers begin their journey toward Pigne d'Arolla. **ABOVE:** The cozy living space, with board games and even a piano to keep guests entertained.

CABANE DES VIGNETTES

REFUGE DES BOUQUETINS

A rustic octagonal bivouac offering breathtaking views of the heart of the Pennine Alps

LOCATION
EVOLÈNE, SWITZERLAND

COORDINATES
45.970863, 7.530535

ALTITUDE
2,980 M (9,777 FT)

ACCESS
4 HOURS

ACCESSIBILITY
YEAR-ROUND

TYPE
BIVOUAC

SLEEPS
20 PEOPLE

POINTS OF INTEREST
**MONT COLLON (3,637 M / 11,932 FT)
MONT BRULÉ (3,578 M / 11,739 FT)
HAUTE ROUTE**

This rugged and traditional shelter is located on the shoulder of a collection of peaks that share its name, dividing the Swiss and Italian Alps. Several summits surrounding the shelter are over 3,600 m (11,811 ft), the highest of which is Sommet Central at 3,838 m (12,592 ft). The wooden refuge and separate guide hut are elegantly perched overlooking the Arolla Glacier, with views of Mont Collon and the spectacular twin peaks of L'Évêque. It is one of Switzerland's more remote bivouac shelters, unmanned but cozy, providing crucial shelter for climbers and ski tourers navigating the high routes of the Valais, including the Haute Route from Chamonix to Zermatt.

Built in 1980 by the Geneva section of the Swiss Alpine Club, the Refuge des Bouquetins takes its name from the alpine ibex that nimbly traverse the steep ridges and rocky outcrops of the surrounding terrain. Constructed from wood with a sharply pitched metal roof to deflect the weight of winter snow, the hut was built for durability rather than comfort. Inside, a few wooden bunks and two tables offer a place to rest, while a small emergency radio provides a tenuous connection to the outside world. A simple wood-burning stove, well positioned in the center of the hut, affords visitors the rare luxury of effortless warm water and dry socks.

The refuge is positioned at the convergence of some of the most dramatic alpine landscapes in the region. Below it, the ancient tongues of the Ferpècle and Arolla glaciers stretch toward the valleys, their fractured surfaces revealing an ever-shifting world of crevasses and seracs. To the west rises the Dent Blanche (4,357 m / 14,295 ft), one of the most striking and highest peaks of the Alps, while to the south, the looming mass of Mont Collon (3,637 m / 11,932 ft) dominates the horizon. The location is both awe-inspiring and unforgiving, with sudden storms and high winds frequently testing the resilience of those seeking its shelter.

The Refuge des Bouquetins plays a vital role in the classic Haute Route, one of the most famous ski traverses in the world. Stretching 180 kilometers (112 miles) between Chamonix and Zermatt, the Haute Route ski route takes seven or more days to ski, depending on conditions. For those moving between the Vignettes and Schönbiel huts, it offers a critical emergency stop in case of worsening weather.

In summer, it serves as a staging point for climbers tackling Mont Brulé (3,578 m/11,739 ft) or the ascent of the Tête Blanche (3,710 m/12,172 ft). The nearby Col Collon has long been a historical crossing, used by traders and explorers for centuries, now serving as a gateway for modern-day adventurers.

After half a century of steadfast service, the hut bears the quiet scars of countless mountaineers and skiers who have sought refuge within its walls. Weathered yet resolute, it carries the echoes of past adventures etched into its wood. Now, as plans for a full restoration take shape, we stand at the threshold of change—grateful for the memories forged, yet eager to witness the next chapter of this amazing hut.

To spend a night at the Refuge des Bouquetins is to embrace the essence of ski mountaineering in the High Alps. Although without a caretaker or board, the Bouquetins is a simple, cozy stopover packed full of Swiss alpine character, offering profound moments of joyful solitude. For those who reach it, whether battered by the wind or awestruck by the silence, the experience is unforgettable.

ABOVE: The unique octagonal shape makes for the perfect setup, with beds surrounding the warm wood stove and plenty of places to hang wet gear.

RIGHT: Enjoying some fresh mountain air while taking in the scenic view from the outhouse. OPPOSITE: Ski touring through the ice caves of Arolla Glacier.

REFUGE DES BOUQUETINS

BIVOUAC DES PÉRIADES

A tiny wooden cabin perched
on a rocky arête deep
in the Mont Blanc massif

LOCATION
GRAIAN ALPS, FRANCE

COORDINATES
45.874599, 6.960212

ALTITUDE
3,421 M (11,224 FT)

ACCESS
4–5 HOURS

ACCESSIBILITY
YEAR-ROUND

TYPE
BIVOUAC

SLEEPS
2 PEOPLE

POINTS OF INTEREST
BRÈCHE PUISEUX
GLACIER DU MONT MALLET

The iconic Bivouac des Périades is definitely not the largest nor most luxurious hut in the world. However, what it lacks in amenities, it more than makes up for in location and ambiance. It balances precariously on the Les Périades, a complex rocky ridgeline between Mont Mallet (3,989 m/13,087 ft) and Aiguille de Rochefort (4,001 m/13,127 ft). The airy ridge is made up of countless granite spires that tower proudly over complex glaciers in every direction.

The wooden hut, fixed onto a rocky outcrop no wider than a few meters, leaves you all too aware of the impossibly daunting exposure on either side. Yet it is a truly one-of-a-kind night in the mountains, more akin to sleeping on a big wall portaledge than an alpine refuge. Below, the vast expanse of the Mont Mallet Glacier flows like a frozen river, its tortured surface a labyrinth of crevasses and seracs. Above, the jagged skyline presents an ever-changing interplay of shadow and light as well as awe-inspiring views of Mont Blanc and its numerous surrounding giants.

Inside, you'll find two small mattresses for a comfortable night's sleep, a netting fitted to the roof to stow away your most valuable items, and just about enough room for your backpack and mountaineering equipment. There are blankets for warmth; however, with its minimal wooden construction and position well over 3,000 m (9,843 ft), even heartier mountaineers may want to consider bringing a high-loft sleeping bag.

The first iteration of the Périades Bivouac was installed as far back as 1925, a relic of an era when mountaineering was raw and unfiltered, when routes were tested by instinct and endurance. The project was led by Parisian mountaineers Paul Chevalier and Maurice Sauvage, and for many years, the small hut was known as the Paul Chevalier Bivouac. It is difficult to fully comprehend the tenacity it takes to build a shelter in this wild and remote location, years before the first ski lifts were built in France and long before the invention of helicopters. The Bivouac des Périades eventually became the property of the French Alpine Club, which took over its maintenance and upkeep. The club renovated the shelter in 1996, and it soon became a beacon for the ingenuity and resilience of mountain life in Chamonix, despite its small size. The hut became a victim of the ever-increasing

OPPOSITE: A skier prepares to rappel from above the hut on the Brèche Puiseux traverse, a classic Chamonix ski tour.

permafrost melt and was destroyed by a rock collapse in 2019. However, thanks to a successful crowdfunding campaign, it was quickly replaced. Over the decades, the bivouac has stood against the fury of the elements, offering a fleeting reprieve to climbers on the cusp of grand objectives. Those bound for the formidable Périades ridge traverse or the ski descents into the hidden folds of the Vallée Blanche have all found respite within its narrow walls.

Reaching the bivouac requires commitment, whether through the glacial expanse of the Mer de Glace or by the classic ski-mountaineering traverse, the Brèche Puiseux. Either way, it demands a high level of mountaineering experience and climbing equipment. The spectacular Brèche Puiseux involves skiing the Vallée Blanche, climbing 1,200 m (3,937 ft) up to the hut, and rappelling down to ski Mont Mallet Glacier's flanks.

For those who crawl through its tiny doorway, it stands as a beautiful testament to why we spend time in the mountains—a desire not to be comfortable but instead to be tested, humbled, and for a moment, to feel utterly small yet profoundly alive.

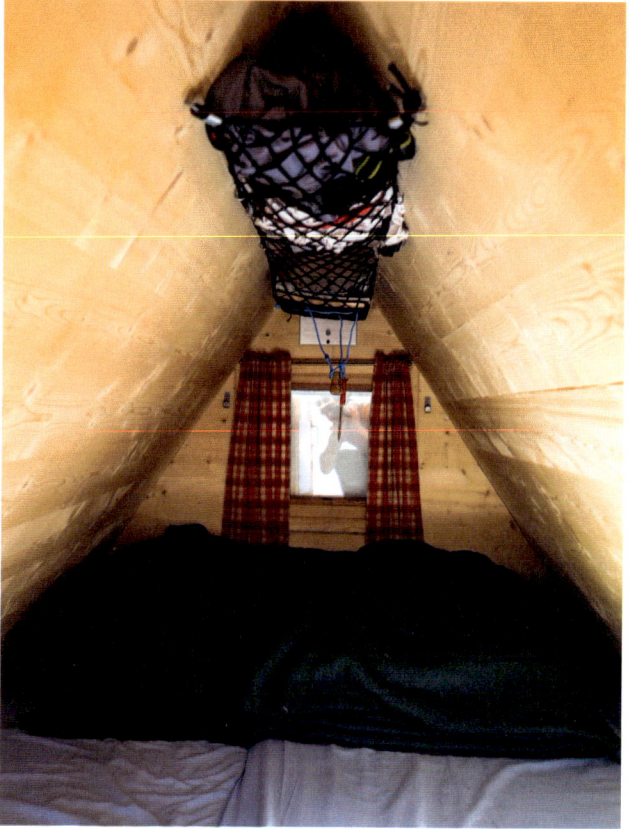

RIGHT: The interior is as basic as it gets, but you'll find a handy storage net for belongings. OPPOSITE: Aiguille Verte dominates the skyline to the north.

SVARTTINDHYTTA

A beautifully classic Scandinavian hut on the remote arctic island of Arnøya

LOCATION
SKJERVØY, NORWAY

COORDINATES
70.156865, 20.598147

ALTITUDE
278 M (912 FT)

ACCESS
1–2 HOURS

ACCESSIBILITY
YEAR-ROUND

TYPE
BIVOUAC

SLEEPS
4 PEOPLE

POINT OF INTEREST
SUMMIT-TO-SEA SKI TOURING & HIKING

Amid the wild, wind-scoured beauty of Norway's far north, where the Arctic Ocean surges against rugged coastlines and the sky stretches vast and unbroken, lies Svarttindhytta. Tucked into the mountainous heart of Arnøya, this cozy refuge is a beacon for those who seek true solitude, adventure, and the unfiltered essence of arctic Norway. Here, the land is raw and unforgiving, but within the walls of the hut, there is warmth, respite, and a deep connection to where mountains meet the sea.

Arnøya, one of Norway's most remote islands, is a place where nature still rules above all. Located 70 degrees north and with a population of only a few hundred people concentrated in the small villages on the coastline, the mountainous interior provides an opportunity to experience true wilderness and a level of solitude hard to come by in the modern world. Arnøyhøgda (1,170 m/3,839 ft), the highest peak on the island, is surrounded by other snow-laden peaks that rise abruptly from the sea, their flanks carved by glaciers long disappeared.

To reach Svarttindhytta, one must earn the privilege—skinning across frozen valleys, navigating rolling hills, and battling the arctic elements, which invariably involve a howling wind and flurries of snow. Departing the small coastal village of Årviksand, there's a tangible sense you're at the edge of civilization as the Arctic Ocean crashes onto the snowy beach. It is a place assured to rouse deep survival instincts and a true sense of adventure. Then, at last, the hut appears—a low, sturdy structure built not to dominate the landscape but to endure it. Its simple red-painted wooden frame, dark against the luminous snow, stands out from the mountainside and yet also belongs. Inside, the scent of pine and melted wax lingers, the walls holding stories of past visitors, their laughter and stories of adventure absorbed into the very grain of the wood.

Built by volunteers and not a part of the extensive Norwegian DNT hut network, Svarttindhytta is a stand-alone hut open to the public and a testament to this close-knit community on Arnøya. Inside, you'll find a wood-burning stove, comfortable bunk beds, and all the cooking equipment needed for a warm meal in the wilderness. The hut is maintained through collective effort. Supplies arrive by sled or are carried in

by those willing to give back to the place that has given them so much. In the visitor's log, names are scrawled beside brief messages—some triumphant, others weary, all united by the bond of shared experience. Supplies include an abundance of wood and gas, but crucially, there is a unique sense that you're a guest on this island, as opposed to a mere tourist passing by.

The hut is perfectly positioned for those who wish to explore the island's untamed beauty. From its doorstep, ski tourers can ascend the surrounding peaks, tracing elegant lines down slopes that plunge toward the sea. The north-facing aspects hold powder long into the spring, while the vast, rolling plateaus offer endless possibilities for exploration.

Svarttindhytta is a reminder that the best journeys do not end at the summit but in the places where we pause, reflect, and share in something greater than ourselves. It is a home in the arctic vastness, a meeting place for the wind, the snow, and the human spirit. To come here is to be humbled by the immensity of nature yet comforted by the warmth found within four simple walls.

ABOVE: Rafting between Arnøya and Kågen. **OPPOSITE:** The Maursund peaks dominate the landscape on the nearby island of Kågen.

OPPOSITE: Exploring here in winter, you'll likely have the mountains to yourself. RIGHT: The cozy wooden interior has plenty of amenities, including gas and a wood-burning stove.

RIFUGIO PASSO SANTNER

A welcoming and modern-classic refuge in the heart of the Dolomites

LOCATION
BOLZANO, ITALY

COORDINATES
46.456429, 11.618210

ALTITUDE
2,734 M (8,970 FT)

ACCESS
2–3 HOURS

ACCESSIBILITY
JUNE–OCTOBER

TYPE
REFUGE

SLEEPS
40 PEOPLE

POINTS OF INTEREST
**VIA FERRATA SANTNER
ROSENGARTENSPITZE (2,981 M / 9,780 FT)**

Nestled among the endless rocky towers of the Dolomites, the Rifugio Passo Santner lies in the Rosengarten group, a dramatic mountain range defined by its pinkish color. At the beginning and end of each clear day, the limestone walls glow, ignited by endless hues that turn the mountains into something truly unforgettable. Set within this landscape is a compact but beautiful triangular prism-shaped hut that delivers the very essence of the Dolomites, and all with the warm hospitality you'd expect from a South Tyrolean refuge in the north of Italy.

The journey to Rifugio Passo Santner is a pilgrimage through nature's grandeur. Those looking for a more relaxing approach can utilize the lift infrastructure provided by the nearby Carezza ski resort before winding through alpine meadows to higher altitudes and through the Val di Fassa. Those looking for the full *Dolomiti* experience can take the Via Ferrata Santner, an involving mountain route equipped with fixed ladders and cables leading climbers through a symphony of stone right to the hut's welcoming doors.

The hut itself is a harmonious blend of tradition and modern design. Originally constructed in 1956 by the esteemed mountain guide Giulio Gabrielli from Predazzo, it stood as a testament to human resilience against nature's formidable backdrop. After years of closure, a renaissance began in 2018 when Michel Perathoner and Romina Huber undertook the mission to breathe new life into this alpine haven. Their vision culminated in a complete redesign by renowned Bolzano-based Senoner Tammerle Architekten, resulting in a structure that marries contemporary design with alpine vernacular. The architects drew inspiration from the surrounding landscape for its triangular "house of cards" design, which features triangular truss frames and solid wood panels. The wooden framework, sheathed in galvanized sheet metal, mirrors the surrounding peaks, reflecting the ever-changing moods of the mountains. This new eco-conscious iteration, which reopened in the summer of 2023, blends into its landscape while leaving the lightest possible footprint.

Inside, the hut exudes a minimalist warmth. Spruce wood dominates the interior, its raw, unblemished shade offering a deceptively bright and spacious feel. The expansive glass facade invites the outside in, offering panoramic views that stretch from the Latemar group to the distant Swiss and Austrian Alps. As sunlight filters through, it

RIFUGIO PASSO SANTNER

bathes the dining area in a golden glow, blurring the lines between shelter and wilderness.

The Rifugio Passo Santner is not merely a place to rest; it is a gateway to adventure. Situated beneath the Rosengarten peak, the second highest in the Rosengarten group, it offers unparalleled access to a myriad of climbing routes and via ferratas. The proximity to the legendary Vajolet Towers beckons climbers to test their mettle against these iconic spires. For those seeking a gentler communion with nature, the surrounding trails provide ample hiking opportunities to immerse oneself in the serene beauty of the Dolomites.

As dusk descends, the phenomenon of alpenglow enshrouds the landscape. The mountains blush with hues of fiery red and soft purple, a daily homage to the legend of King Laurin and his cursed rose garden for which the range shares its name. According to legend, it is here, amid these peaks, that the king's enchanted roses bloom eternally in the twilight, painting the mountains with their ephemeral glow.

Within the hut, the spirit of community thrives. Michel, tending to the kitchen, crafts dishes that are a contemporary ode to Tyrolean cuisine, each bite a fusion of tradition and innovation. Romina's presence in the dining area adds a personal touch, her warmth reflecting the very essence of alpine hospitality. Together, they have cultivated an atmosphere where stories are exchanged over hearty meals, laughter echoes against wooden walls, and strangers become companions united by the mountains.

The Rifugio Passo Santner stands as a beacon for those who seek both the challenge of the ascent and the solace of refuge. It embodies the delicate balance between comfort and the surrounding rugged mountainscapes, offering a haven where one can reflect, rejuvenate, and revel in the timeless allure of the Dolomites.

OPPOSITE: The angular galvanized steel exterior of Rifugio Passo Santner stands out perfectly against the moon-like geology of the Dolomites.

ABOVE: Large windows and light wood give the hut's interior a beautifully bright and spacious feel. OPPOSITE: The refuge offers access to the iconic towering walls of the Rosengarten.

JIM HABERL HUT

A welcoming and comfortable refuge nestled in Canada's Tantalus Range

LOCATION
SQUAMISH, CANADA

COORDINATES
49.796716, −123.311459

ALTITUDE
2,030 M (6,660 FT)

ACCESS
14 HOURS

ACCESSIBILITY
MARCH–SEPTEMBER

TYPE
REFUGE

SLEEPS
12 PEOPLE

POINTS OF INTEREST
**MOUNT TANTALUS (2,603 M / 8,540 FT)
MOUNT DIONE (2,590 M / 8,497 FT)
ALPHA MOUNTAIN (2,305 M / 7,562 FT)**

Tucked into the granite spine of the Tantalus Range, the Jim Haberl Hut occupies a perch so wild and defiantly remote that reaching the hut itself is a feat of stoic endurance. It rests just below 2,000 m (6,562 ft) on the flanks of Serratus Mountain, where rock gives way to glaciers, and clouds drift close to the ridgelines. This is not a hut stumbled upon; it is earned. Built against the elements, it stands like a pause in the wilderness: a place to exhale after hours of upward effort through tangled forest and alpine stone.

The hut is compact, solid, and purposeful. Although primarily built to endure the surrounding mountains, it undoubtedly decorates the landscape as well. The unique teal hue contrasts starkly with the orange wooden shutters and surrounding rocky gray spurs. Its corrugated steel sides gleam dully in sunlight and fade into grayscale under clouds. The sharply pitched roof, almost A-frame in profile, sheds heavy snow with ease, and its elevated position on a rocky bench gives it sweeping views in nearly every direction. A small deck fronts the entrance, often used to stomp off snow or rest packs after a long climb or ski.

Inside, the atmosphere is spartan and yet comforting. The main room is a combination of a kitchen, dining area, and drying zone. A long bench-lined table provides space for shared meals and route planning by headlamp glow. Hooks and drying lines crisscross the ceiling, typically draped with damp layers steaming gently beside the wood-burning stove. The kitchen is equipped with countertops, basic utensils, cookware, and a propane system for cooking—minimal yet functional, intended only for self-reliant mountaineers.

Sleeping quarters are divided across two loft-style areas with padded sleeping platforms, accommodating around 12 people. There's no privacy, but that's part of the charm: a shared space where stories echo, laughter lingers, and the fatigue of the day is softened by eventual communal stillness. Windows look out over the surrounding peaks, framing sunsets and snowstorms with equal drama.

The approach in summer most often begins from the Sigurd Creek trailhead. The path climbs steeply through a damp, green cathedral of cedar and hemlock, the air thick with moss and the scent of rain-soaked loam. Higher up, the forest thins, replaced by avalanche

gullies and scree fields, where the route becomes more rugged and indistinct. Navigation demands attention, and the sense of remoteness runs deep with every step. Eventually, the trail breaks into the alpine realm of glacier-fed tarns, wind-stunted heather, and silence. By the time the hut appears, cradled against a backdrop of broken peaks and blue ice, the world below feels a distant memory.

In late winter and early spring, the hut transforms into a beacon for ski mountaineers. Some arrive by helicopter drop; others brave long, demanding ascents from the Squamish Valley or Lake Lovely Water. The range is transfigured—sharp ridges softened under snow, glaciers blanketed in white, couloirs beckoning with cold promise. The hut itself may be half-buried, a single door dug out, its windows rimmed with frost. But inside, boots steam by the fire and skis rest against the wall, and the atmosphere glows with shared relief. From here, strong parties can access serious ski terrain: the east face of Serratus, Rumbling Glacier, or multiday traverses that demand precision and respect.

The hut was built in memory of Jim Haberl—a Canadian alpinist, photojournalist, and mountain guide—who died in an avalanche in Alaska in 1999. Haberl was one of the first Canadians to reach the summit of K2, the famous mountain on the border between Pakistan and China. His passion for wild places and his gift for sharing their stories live on here in wood, stone, and sky. This is a shelter born not just of practicality but of passion for the mountains and those who move through them.

Evenings settle slowly in this high place. A meal shared. Gear drying in quiet heaps. The sound of wind slipping over remains of snowfields. Whether in boots or skis, sun or storm, those who reach the Jim Haberl Hut arrive changed, not because the mountains welcomed them, but because they made room within them. And here, held in that stillness, they find what every great hut offers: not escape but true belonging in the wilderness.

OPPOSITE: The vivid rust-red and pine-green colors of the Jim Haberl Hut contrast with the surrounding snow-covered slopes.

OPPOSITE: The Tantalus Range rises sharply above Squamish with glaciated peaks and steep ridgelines characteristic of the Coast Mountains.

KVERKFJÖLL MOUNTAIN HUT

A remote outpost at the juncture of ice and fire

LOCATION
VATNAJÖKULL NATIONAL PARK, ICELAND

COORDINATES
64.672500, −16.689750

ALTITUDE
1,718 M (5,636 FT)

ACCESS
1 DAY (4 × 4 + 3 HOURS HIKING)

ACCESSIBILITY
YEAR-ROUND

TYPE
BIVOUAC

SLEEPS
6–12 PEOPLE

POINTS OF INTEREST
KVERKFJÖLL (1,860 M / 6,102 FT)
SKARPHÉÐINSTINDUR (1,944 M / 6,378 FT)

Established at the remote edge of Iceland's interior, where fire meets ice in a furious embrace, the Kverkfjöll Mountain Hut is one of the country's most isolated. Iceland itself straddles the Mid-Atlantic Ridge, one of the few places on Earth where tectonic plates visibly diverge, forging a restless, ever-forming land of glaciers, lava fields, and steaming vents. The hut stands as a weatherworn sentinel on the northern flanks of the Vatnajökull ice cap—the largest glacier in Europe—watching over a landscape shaped by subterranean heat and glacial forces. Here, in this barren yet striking landscape, the world is diluted to the simplest of elements: wind, snow, and silence.

The Kverkfjöll Mountain Hut is modest, practical, and deeply resilient—qualities befitting its environment. A low-slung, wood-framed structure braced against the howling winds, it offers sturdy shelter to those bold enough to journey into this wild volcanic frontier. The roof, frequently scoured by snow and ash, carries the texture of countless storms. Inside, rough-hewn bunk beds line the walls, a gas-burning stove stands ready to push back the arctic chill, and a communal table invites the exchange of shared hardship and awe.

Kverkfjöll is an active volcanic range rising directly from beneath the glacier. The hut sits just outside the mouth of the Kverkjökull outlet glacier, a frozen river pouring from a caldera laced with geothermal vents and steaming ice caves. This paradoxical zone of heat and ice has drawn scientists, mountaineers, and dreamers for decades. From the hut, routes fan out across the glacier for high ski touring in spring and early summer, and deep into the glacier's mysterious ice caves in winter—always with a cautious eye on the volatile geology below.

Historically, the hut has served as both a basecamp for scientific exploration and a waystation for adventurers pushing into the island's central highlands. Managed by the Iceland Glaciological Society, it reflects a long tradition of scientific tenacity against the elements in Iceland's inhospitable heart. Early expeditions here sought to understand glacial movements and volcanic phenomena. Today, the same spirit of inquiry and endurance endures in every climber who straps on skis or crampons and ventures upward.

Reaching Kverkfjöll requires planning, patience, and≈a healthy respect for the unpredictable. In summer, seasoned drivers with capable 4×4 vehicles can follow rough interior tracks that snake through the Ódáðahraun lava desert—an unforgiving landscape of black rock, ancient myth, and absolute silence. In winter, the approach is even more formidable, with multiday ski or snowmobile journeys beginning from outposts like Möðrudalur or Askja. Weather, route-finding, and glacial conditions can shift swiftly, and self-reliance in this rapidly changeable environment is essential. Those, however, who do come prepared are rewarded with the extraordinary. Despite the remoteness, or perhaps because of it, Kverkfjöll exudes a kind of sacred stillness. It is a place to witness the earth's rawest equilibriums: creation and destruction, solitude and connection, danger and divinity.

ABOVE: In true Icelandic style, ice meets fire at the Grímsvötn hut, a rare outpost in Vatnajökull National Park.

SEFTON BIVOUAC

An elemental, historic shelter in the heart of New Zealand's Aoraki/Mount Cook National Park

LOCATION
CANTERBURY, NEW ZEALAND

COORDINATES
−43.687824, 170.075905

ALTITUDE
1,650 M (5,413 FT)

ACCESS
3–5 HOURS

ACCESSIBILITY
YEAR-ROUND

TYPE
BIVOUAC

SLEEPS
4 PEOPLE

POINTS OF INTEREST
MOUNT SEFTON (3,151 M / 10,338 FT)
MOUNT BRUNNER (2,643 M / 8,671 FT)

Perched on a wind-raked spur above the Hooker Valley in the heart of New Zealand's Southern Alps, Sefton Bivouac stands alone in a realm where the land rules itself. This is true wilderness—a place of elemental power, where weather shapes the day and human presence is fleeting. Its scarlet corrugated shell clings to the mountainside at over 1,600 m (5,249 ft), beneath the shattered icefalls of Mount Sefton. There is no easy path to this place. Reached by a steep, unmarked scramble through scree and alpine tussock, the bivvy rewards only those who come prepared to listen to the silence and move with the grain of the land.

The approach to the hut is a test of resolve in and of itself. There is no marked trail, only a faint route that veers sharply uphill from the Hooker Valley Track, ascending through draped ribbons of mountain daisy and spear grass. The terrain grows austere as you rise, with sweeping views unfolding over the colossal Mueller Glacier, Hooker Valley, and distant Aoraki itself. When the hut finally reveals itself, perched precariously on a rocky outcrop, there is no shortage of alpine drama here, with mountain scenery that can compete with anywhere else in the world.

The bivouac is brazen—its bright orange-red walls popping boldly against the blue glacier ice that hangs above. Like many modest huts in New Zealand, there is no fee for staying overnight, and sleeping arrangements are available on a first-come, first-served basis. Inside, you'll find four bunks but no stove, no insulation, and no frills. Yet there is a raw beauty to its austerity. It smells faintly of cold metal and alpine dreams. The floor creaks. Here, the walls hold over a century of stories—of stormbound nights, sunrise ascents, and quiet meals shared in the hush of moonlight. Every visitor adds something intangible to its fabric. One cannot help but feel part of a long and quiet existence.

Built in 1917, the Sefton Bivouac is thought to be New Zealand's oldest-surviving alpine hut. Its original purpose was to support climbers tackling Mount Sefton and nearby peaks—ambitious climbers in wool and hobnail boots who carved their legends into the snow. In those early days, the shelter was a crucial foothold in a time when alpine access for these pioneers was neither simple nor safe. The fact that it endures, largely unchanged, is a modest act of reverence.

OPPOSITE: Despite its relatively modest altitude, the Sefton Bivouac offers glaciated drama and towering peaks.

Today, the Sefton Bivouac is a relic and a refuge—a link to the golden age of New Zealand mountaineering, of course, becoming renowned for its part in the first ascent of Mount Everest. It's hard not to imagine a young Sir Edmund Hillary forging his alpine skills here in his formative years. A dedicated statue and alpinism museum in the valley below celebrate his remarkable alpine adventures.

While its practical use has waned with the rise of helicopters and modern high-altitude huts, it remains a coveted destination for purists, romantics, and those seeking solitude in the raw company of the mountains. For ski tourers, it can be an ambitious waypoint, though access in winter is treacherous and tests experience. Few places on Earth offer a dawn like Sefton's, where the first light strikes the fluted face of the mountain and spills molten gold across the glacier-scored valley. In those moments, the bivvy becomes more than shelter; it becomes a chapel, lookout, and time capsule. To stay here is to commune with the mountain in its own language—brief, elemental, and unforgettable.

SEFTON BIVOUAC

GRASSENBIWAK

A small, traditional, well-equipped hut on the edge of one of Switzerland's favorite freeride-ski resorts

LOCATION
ENGELBERG, SWITZERLAND

COORDINATES
46.770203, 8.446646

ALTITUDE
2,647 M (8,684 FT)

ACCESS
4–6 HOURS

ACCESSIBILITY
YEAR-ROUND

TYPE
BIVOUAC

SLEEPS
18 PEOPLE

POINTS OF INTEREST
**TITLIS (3,238 M / 10,623 FT)
TITLIS RUNDTOUR
URNER HAUTE ROUTE**

Just beyond the bustle of Engelberg, where gondolas hum and slopes carve their winter lines, the mountains shift. The terrain steepens, the crowds vanish, and the wilderness takes over. Tucked neatly below the vast Titlis wall—like a secret kept just out of sight—the Grassenbiwak lies in startling solitude. Though only a ridgeline or two away from the resort, it feels a world removed. Here, above 2,600 m (8,530 ft), you cross an invisible threshold: from the ordered domain of ski infrastructure into the raw, radiant gateway to the Urner Alps. This is a landscape of towering snowy peaks and glaciers littered with seracs, where the Grassenbiwak marks the edge of familiarity and the beginning of something far wilder.

The hut is a small, polygonal wooden structure—weathered and faceted like a pine cone caught between boulders. Its dark wood blends into the surrounding rocky landscape, unassuming yet sturdy, shaped to deflect wind and snow rather than invite comfort. Inside, the furnishings are simple but cozy: a wall of wooden bunks can host more people than would be comfortable, a compact wood-burning stove for warmth effortlessly melts snow, and a shared table where headlamps flicker in the early hours of an alpine start. Most crucially, however, Grassenbiwak is bustling with character and unique touches, a plentiful supply of wood stored in the basement, an unusual array of dining utensils, and even the opportunity to purchase a bottle of wine from the well-stocked wine cellar. The walls, thick with years of stickers, etched initials, and mountaineers' scribbled entries, hum with the quiet company of those who've passed through.

One of the more adventurous ways to reach the Grassenbiwak is via the Titlis Rundtour. This classic ski mountaineering circuit loops elegantly through some of the most breathtaking alpine terrain in the area. From the highest lift-served point above Engelberg, soft turns unfold on cold, north-facing snow before the journey swings west, weaving through the jagged skyline of the Titlisjoch. A dramatic mix of steep couloirs and ski rappels carries you deeper into the alpine unknown, each descent revealing wilder ground. Finally, the Wenden Glacier rises ahead, and with a last, steady climb, the route crests the col where the Grassenbiwak waits, quiet and steadfast.

In the morning, there are infinite itineraries for those looking for yet more adventure, or a superb 1,500-m (4,921-ft) glacier ski descent right from the door that takes you back to the Engelberg Valley.

The Grassenbiwak is also a popular stop on the Urner Haute Route. This iconic ski traverse of the Urner Alps stretches from Andermatt to Engelberg and typically takes five days. Whatever the route for ski tourers, the Grassenbiwak is both a milestone and a moment of pause. Ski touring in the area is by no means trivial—crevasse navigation, avalanche terrain, and steep passages require a high level of skill and experience. And yet, the Urner Alps are beloved for their rugged beauty: the sculpted ice of the surrounding four glaciers, the morning light striking the Mährenhorn on the horizon, and the Titlis face, which appears as though it would be more at home in Yosemite.

Built in 1970 by the Swiss Alpine Club, the Grassenbiwak was placed with purpose. It offers a safe harbor in this otherwise exposed alpine crossing, especially vital in bad weather or late in the day when retreat could be complicated. In summer, climbers use the bivouac as a base for ascents of Grassen (2,946 m/ 9,665 ft), Wendenhorn (3,023 m/9,918 ft), and many more. Though the approaches are longer on foot, the spirit of the place remains the same.

The Grassenbiwak is full of character—thoughtfully built, quietly welcoming, and far more than just a place to wait out the night. Being here grants a palpable sense of feeling small and yet welcome. Inside, the space feels unexpectedly warm and lived-in, as though you're a guest in a mountain home, not just a mountaineer seeking shelter. The wood creaks softly, the stove radiates comfort, and every detail, from the handwritten notes to the careful arrangement of gear, speaks of the many who've passed through with care and respect. On the cusp of the wilderness of the Urner Alps, this hidden gem offers not just safety but a rare sense of belonging.

OPPOSITE: The mountains beyond the hut offer countless ski-touring opportunities, such as the famed Urner Haute Route.

ABOVE: The bivouac boasts a traditional but surprisingly well-equipped kitchen and living space. **OPPOSITE:** The Titlis wall stands as an ever-impressive backdrop.

CABANE TORTIN

A mountain hut experience at the summit of luxury and sophistication

LOCATION
HAUTE-NENDAZ, SWITZERLAND

COORDINATES
46.084864, 7.311450

ALTITUDE
2,992 M (9,816 FT)

ACCESS
SKI LIFT

ACCESSIBILITY
ADVANCED BOOKINGS ONLY; OPEN DECEMBER–APRIL

TYPE
HOTEL

SLEEPS
8 PEOPLE

POINTS OF INTEREST
**MONT FORT (3,328 M / 10,919 FT)
BEC DES ETAGNES (3,232 M / 10,604 FT)**

Tucked into a high-alpine bowl above the Val de Bagnes, where the air thins and the silence deepens, Cabane Tortin emerges like a mirage—half mountain dream, half modern marvel. At just shy of 3,000 m (9,843 ft) above sea level, where most huts offer only the barest reprieve from the elements, Tortin extends a hand wrapped in cashmere. This all-new mountain sanctuary offers the benefits one could expect from a traditional alpine refuge, without having to forego luxuries that would be expected in the most lavish of chalets. At the Tortin, luxury meets wilderness in this unique high-alpine offering.

From the moment one crests the final rise, boots crunching on wind-scoured snow, legs heavy from a big day of lift-access freeride on the slopes of Verbier and Nendaz—Cabane Tortin glows like a beacon. Its sleek wood and minimalist concrete silhouette rests with sophisticated confidence against a backdrop of glaciated summits: the Bec des Etagnes to the west, the jagged Mont Fort just above, and a sweep of spurs and cols in between. The structure honors alpine tradition with its low, wind-shedding roofline. Yet, the details are unmistakably contemporary: solar-powered electricity, an ever-impressive panoramic glass facade, and interiors scented with larch and the faintest trace of cedar.

Inside, the hut exudes a warmth rare at this altitude—both literally and figuratively. Contemporary furniture is lined with plush wool throws and the walls with curated alpine art. Communal spaces invite weary ski tourers to sink into armchairs with views that span across the Valais region. Evenings can be effortlessly filled chatting in front of the fire, relaxing those weary legs in the sauna, or enjoying a bottle of red from a wine list more at home in a Michelin-starred restaurant than a high-altitude cabin. Meals are a revelation: the in-house team serves cocktails and canapés, ensuring that dinner is the perfect crescendo concluding each day.

But Cabane Tortin is not just a haven of elegance, it is an exclusive outpost nestled atop one of the Alps' most famed freeride and ski-touring areas. From here, bold lines beckon across untouched snowfields and rarely trodden ridgelines. The Glacier de Tortin unfurls below, providing sweeping backcountry descents toward Siviez and Verbier and fresh tracks down untouched corduroy slopes for those looking to stay

OPPOSITE AND ABOVE: With its luxurious interior, modern panoramic windows, and expansive stone terrace, this is not your average mountain stay.

inbounds. Avalanche courses, high-alpine navigation workshops, and backcountry-guide gatherings often converge here, elevating the refuge to more than just a resting point. Cabane Tortin has dedicated mountain guides, and with them, an opportunity for alpine learning and shared adventure.

Historically, this site was once no more than a shepherd's summer bivouac, later fortified by skipatrollers and guides who saw the need for a mid-mountain station in the sprawling 4 Vallées terrain. It wasn't until recently, with a bold vision and rare investment, that Cabane Tortin was reborn into one of the highest privately owned and managed mountain huts. In doing so, it has become a one-of-a-kind experience. Naturally, a stay with this much finesse won't fit into everyone's budget, but creating a space with such extraordinary comfort within the high-alpine panorama is a rare testament to human ingenuity and design. In the quiet hours before dawn, when stars scatter like frost across the sky and the wind brushes the walls like a whisper, Cabane Tortin reminds you: the mountains can be merciless, but they can also be kind.

CABANE TORTIN

ABOVE: Never-ending sunsets and relaxing vibes grace the Cabane Tortin long after the other skiers have returned to the resorts.

BIVAK II NA JEZERIH

A silver sentinel in the heart of Slovenia's Southern Limestone Alps

LOCATION
TRIGLAV NATIONAL PARK, SLOVENIA

COORDINATES
46.433625, 13.838607

ALTITUDE
2,118 M (6,949 FT)

ACCESS
2–3 HOURS

ACCESSIBILITY
YEAR-ROUND

TYPE
BIVOUAC

SLEEPS
6 PEOPLE

POINT OF INTEREST
VODNIKOV VRŠAC (2,118 M / 6,949 FT)

Positioned among some of the highest peaks in the Julian Alps, at the edge of the Triglav National Park's rawest wilderness, Bivak II na Jezerih is a simple shelter cast of aluminum and wood. Perched on a plateau at over 2,000 m (6,562 ft), this humble refuge gazes across a horizon of limestone ridges and tumbling scree, standing sentinel over a realm shaped by glaciers, time, and solitude. The bivouac is a small, unmanned shelter—austere in its amenities but profound in its purpose. Its corrugated aluminum skin gleams in the alpine sun, burnished by wind and weather, resilient against the storms that sweep through these dramatic mountains. Inside, the hut is a capsule of calm: six sleeping berths, a wooden bench, a modest table, and an alpine register filled with the scribbled confessions of wanderers. No stove, no running water, no electricity—only the purity of mountain silence and the comfort of a roof between climber and ever-changing skies.

The original wooden hut was built in 1934, one of the earliest bivouacs in Slovenia's high mountains, a tribute to the country's enduring mountaineering spirit. Raised by volunteers from the Skala Mountaineering Club, the bivouac was conceived as a lifeline for climbers tackling the demanding faces of the surrounding peaks. Constructed of lightweight aluminum for easy transport, the current iteration was delivered by helicopter. While unique in character, it still adheres to the beautiful minimalist design standards you'd expect from a modern Slovenian hut. During the day, when the sun is high, its metal facade gleams, standing proudly against the bright blue skies and washed-out limestone cliffs. In the early mornings and evenings, however, the hut is painted in the orange and pink hues of alpenglow, blending harmoniously into the surrounding landscape. Today, it remains a vital waypoint on high-alpine and ski-touring routes, offering sanctuary amid the stark beauty of these alpine pastures.

To reach it is to surrender to the landscape. Most approach from Planina Blato, a circular hiking trail that winds through pastures, forests, and high karst valleys before climbing the stony switchbacks into the realm of the ibex and chough. The trail, though not technically difficult in good weather, demands stamina and a reverent demeanor. It is a journey where every step carries you further from modern life.

In winter, the bivouac becomes a hidden gem for ski tourers seeking wild lines in quiet terrain. The surrounding slopes—often laden with deep snow and framed by toothy ridgelines—offer adventurous descents far from the bustle of the better-known Triglav routes. The bivouac itself, half-buried in snowdrifts, becomes a precious, glowing capsule where steaming breath and hot tea feel like the only luxuries one needs.

There is something monastic about a night spent here. The stars burn brighter in this high silence, and the wind carries stories from summit to summit. You feel the presence of others—those who have come before, seeking shelter, inspiration, or a way through the storm. In the logbook, you may find a poem, a warning, or a sketch of the surrounding peaks—traces of the quiet camaraderie that bind this now-international alpine tribe.

Here, high above the forests and meadows, Bivak II na Jezerih invites climbers to step into Slovenia's rich mountaineering legacy and lose themselves in the fierce splendor of the Julian Alps—a range whose stature may be modest but whose spirit towers high.

OPPOSITE: The unique bell-shaped construction can withstand 200-km/h winds.
ABOVE: The beautiful wooden interior is archetypical of Slovenian bivouacs.

RIGHT: Looking out from the summit of Veliki Oltar (2,621 m) to the ever-impressive Triglav National Park, even more spectacular in the winter months.

BIVAK NA PREHODAVCIH

A discrete and essential shelter deep in Triglav National Park

LOCATION
TRIGLAV NATIONAL PARK, SLOVENIA

COORDINATES
46.358090, 13.792288

ALTITUDE
2,071 M (6,795 FT)

ACCESS
4–5 HOURS

ACCESSIBILITY
YEAR-ROUND

TYPE
BIVOUAC

SLEEPS
24 PEOPLE

POINTS OF INTEREST
POPROVEC (2,496 M / 8,189 FT)
VELIKO ŠPIČJE (2,398 M / 7,867 FT)

High in Slovenia's Julian Alps, near a confluence of key mountaineering routes, sits the Bivak na Prehodavcih—a simple yet vital refuge at over 2,000 m (6,562 ft). Associated with the nearby Zasavska Koča summer refuge, this bivouac is an essential shelter for climbers, hikers, and ski tourers traversing the rugged heart of Triglav National Park in the off-season. Though modest in structure, its role in providing protection and access to some of the region's most challenging terrain for eight months of the year makes it a cornerstone of alpine life in the area.

Built for necessity rather than comfort, the bivouac offers little beyond its essential gifts: a sturdy roof, protective walls, and the immeasurable peace of knowing that, for one night, you are safe in the arms of the mountains. The unassuming design features a narrow concrete base, the remains of a former First World War bunker. Triangular corrugated metal walls extend from the base, allowing this minimalist hut to blend effortlessly into the surrounding rocky slopes, as if it grew from the mountain itself. Its asymmetric design helps the bivouac withstand strong alpine wind year-round and offers natural snow-shedding capabilities in winter.

Stepping into the bivouac after a long day's climb is like entering a sacred space. The scent of pine boards, faint and comforting, lingers in the cool air. There are narrow sleeping platforms with mattresses and bedding, a wooden table worn smooth by the passage of countless hands, and a window that frames the sky's shifting moods—cobalt blue at midday, searing gold at sunset, a wash of stars in the cold alpine night. Every scratch on the floorboards, every name carved into a beam, is a whispered testament to those who have chosen to experience adventure here.

The surroundings are stark and unforgettable. Jagged peaks of Triglav National Park stretch in every direction, their pale limestone faces etched with the marks of wind, snow, and time. In late summer, pockets of edelweiss and hardy alpine grasses stubbornly cling to life in the cracks. In winter, snow lays a deep and silent mantle over the world, smoothing out the ruggedness but deepening the sense of remote isolation.

The history of Bivak na Prehodavcih is deeply intertwined with Slovenia's long-standing alpine tradition

and the spirit of communal mountain stewardship. The bivouac was established as an auxiliary shelter to the larger Zasavska Koča. It was built in 1954 by a local mountaineering club to support the growing number of climbers exploring the high routes of the Julian Alps. These shelters are acts of collective devotion, born from countless volunteer hours and a stubborn belief that the mountains should remain open to all. Over the decades, the need for a year-round emergency shelter became clear, until the hut we see today was renovated in 2013, offering refuge for numerous intrepid mountaineers and skiers throughout the winter. The entire structure was manufactured and preassembled in the valley, then transported piecemeal by helicopter and reassembled on-site.

The bivouac is more than just a waypoint; it is a vital artery for mountaineers and ski tourers who venture into this high country. Reaching the hut alone involves a challenging 1,400-m (4,593-ft) climb, serving as a crucial access point to some of the Julian Alps' most demanding and rewarding routes—from the lofty summits of Kanjavec to countless other 2,000-m (6,562-ft) peaks. There is no shortage of ski touring options in the area, with a sweeping descent back down the Trenta Valley, or for the more adventurous, the opportunity to go deeper into Triglav National Park, connecting with multiple huts along the way. When poor weather strikes, the bivouac can mean the difference between a life saved and tragedy in this unforgiving and complex terrain.

Here, amid the endless sky and rugged limestone cliffs, Bivak na Prehodavcih is an essential cornerstone for great journeys in the spectacular Julian Alps. From its humble shelter, climbers and ski tourers launch themselves into some of Slovenia's wildest, most demanding terrain, each step a dialogue with the elements. In the quiet between summits and storms, the bivouac stands firm—a small but vital guardian of human ambition in the high mountains all year round.

OPPOSITE: The raised entrance allows access during even the snowiest months, and the angular design blends seamlessly into the surroundings.

RIGHT: Inside, the clean minimalist design has plenty of beds for a bivouac of this size. OPPOSITE: Two skiers take in the last vivid sunset hues.

BIVAK NA PREHODAVCIH

REFUGE DES GRANDS MULETS

A historic refuge precariously perched in the heart of the Mont Blanc massif

LOCATION
CHAMONIX, FRANCE

COORDINATES
45.866605, 6.861033

ALTITUDE
3,051 M (10,010 FT)

ACCESS
3–4 HOURS

ACCESSIBILITY
APRIL–JULY

TYPE
REFUGE

SLEEPS
68 PEOPLE

POINT OF INTEREST
MONT BLANC (4,806 M / 15,768 FT)

The Refuge des Grands Mulets is positioned strategically on the northern glaciated flanks of Western Europe's highest peak, Mont Blanc. The vibrant night-lit streets of Chamonix can be seen in the depths of the valley below, and though not technically remote, it feels a long way from civilization. The pyramidal rock island on which the refuge is perched is surrounded by an unforgiving labyrinth of ever-changing ice from two interlacing streams of the Bossons Glacier. Time moves differently here, governed by the slow, imperceptible flow of glacial ice and the periodic, rapid, and unpredictable sounds of collapsing seracs. It is a place that commands respect—both for its wildness and for the unwavering role it plays in the story of Mont Blanc.

The Refuge des Grands Mulets is an essential stopover for those undertaking the ski ascent of Mont Blanc, a route that blends history and an unshakable tenacity for this grand massif. The hut itself is simple yet steadfast, clinging to the exposed rock as if bracing against the weight of the elements. Inside, wooden bunks line the walls, and the air hums with the quiet rituals of alpinism—boots stamping off snow, whispered route plans, the hiss of a stove boiling water for tea. At night, the wind rattles against the walls, a reminder of the wilderness that presses in on all sides.

The history of the Refuge des Grands Mulets is inseparable from the history of Mont Blanc itself. It was on these slopes, in 1786, that Jacques Balmat and Michel-Gabriel Paccard pioneered the first ascent of Mont Blanc, their route weaving between icefalls and exposed ridges, guided only by instinct and a will to discover this mountain's secrets. This feat is heralded as the beginning of modern alpinism. Chamonix native Marie Paradis was the first woman to summit Mont Blanc in 1808 at the age of 18. So fatigued by the climb after summiting, she begged her male companions to throw her into the nearest crevasse to end her misery. Luckily, she found the resolve to make it back down.

The first rudimentary shelter in the area appeared in 1853, marking the site as an essential waypoint for those who would follow in their footsteps. Over the decades, the structure evolved to meet the needs of modern mountaineers, but its purpose remains unchanged— a place to pause, to prepare for a summit push, to take refuge in a world where few places offer it.

Today, the Grands Mulets route remains the popular choice for ski mountaineers seeking to summit Mont Blanc. In the spring, snow covers deep crevasses—prime conditions for one of the longest continuous ski descents in the Alps. From the refuge, the route climbs toward the Petit Plateau and Grand Plateau, vast snowy expanses dwarfed by the soaring ice cliffs of Mont Blanc's north face. The ascent is equally magnificent as it is committing, each step demanding careful route-finding through this network of snow and ice. Even for experienced ski mountaineers, the route is long and physically demanding, forcing many groups to depart from the hut as early as midnight, unlikely to be finished before the afternoon. It is also the most direct route to the summit from Chamonix, a route that's witnessed the likes of Kilian Jornet and Hillary Gerardi racing to the top and back to town in only 4 hours, 57 minutes and 7 hours, 25 minutes, respectively.

The lucky ones will reach the summit at dawn when the mountains glow with ethereal light, the rising sun igniting the upper slopes in soft hues of rose and gold. It is in these fleeting moments, when the world is painted in alpenglow and silence, that the grandeur of the place is truly felt. After that, it's time to clip in and ski directly from the highest peak in the Alps and, if you're lucky, enjoy north-facing, untracked powder all the way back to the refuge.

Few refuges are as exposed, precarious, or steeped in mountaineering tradition as the Refuge des Grands Mulets. To stay here is to retrace the steps of the pioneers of alpine exploration and in more recent years, of audacious record-breaking speed attempts. It is a place where past and present converge, where history is not merely remembered but relived with every ascent. Those who pass through its doors join a lineage of climbers bound by the same pursuit, the same longing for altitude, and the same quiet awe on the north face of one of Europe's most iconic peaks.

OPPOSITE: Jess Clark skiing the north face of Mont Blanc on a bluebird powder day, a classic descent off the highest peak in the Alps.

OPPOSITE: An early "alpine start" for skiers making their way up to Mont Blanc, a challenging day with over 2,000m of ascent, with the glowing lights of Chamonix below.

REFUGE DES GRANDS MULETS

GAPPOHYTTA

A cluster of Scandinavian cabins nestled between arctic Norway, Finland, and Sweden

LOCATION
STORFJORD, NORWAY

COORDINATES
69.053166, 20.253560

ALTITUDE
706 M (2,316 FT)

ACCESS
2–3 HOURS

ACCESSIBILITY
YEAR-ROUND

TYPE
BIVOUAC

SLEEPS
24 PEOPLE

POINTS OF INTEREST
**THREE-COUNTRY CAIRN
BÁRRÁS (1,419 M / 4,656 FT)
PÄLTSAN (1,442 M / 4,731 FT)**

Perched high and alone in the snow-smoothed folds of the Norwegian-Swedish borderlands, Gappohytta offers refuge in the liminal—between nations, between seasons, between silence and storm. Managed by the Norwegian Trekking Association (DNT), this modest-yet-resolute refuge is nestled at 706 m (2,316 ft) above sea level in the heart of the Signaldalen Valley, a place where the spine of the Lyngen Alps begins to ripple outward into vast arctic plateaus. To arrive here, whether by ski, snowshoe, or on foot, is to pass through corridors of cloud-shadowed birch and up into a high country where the wind carves the snow like a sculptor and time continues to move with glacial grace.

The huts themselves are humble, a collection of weatherworn wooden structures with sloped roofs and red detailing in traditional Scandinavian style. The Old Gappo and New Gappo huts provide plenty of living space and sleeping spots, and a separate annex for dog owners features four beds and dog kennels in the corridor. Another hut is dedicated to compost toilets and an abundant supply of wood. In winter, snow piles high against its flanks, insulating the thick log walls that have sheltered generations of skiers and mountaineers. Inside, the air carries the faint scent of woodsmoke and pine. A black iron stove squats at the center like a hearth heart, radiating warmth that thaws both body and spirit. The bunks are simple, the table scarred by maps and mugs and memories. There is a distinct coziness inside, contrasting perfectly against the beginnings of arctic tundra that lie on the other side of the door, a true sanctuary in the far north.

Gappohytta has expanded over the years. The first cabin, Old Gappo, was built in 1973, followed by New Gappo in 1984, and the dog annex in 2008. The cabins stand as sentinels on the old Sami trails and wartime courier routes that once threaded this rugged border. Its very name—*gappo*, a local term—hints at a pass, a crossing point, a threshold. In summer, it is a waypoint for hikers exploring the Nordkalottleden, a long-distance trail that winds through Norway, Sweden, and Finland. In winter, it becomes a lifeline for ski tourers traversing the great arctic arc between Kåfjord and Kilpisjärvi. The terrain around it is vast and varied: sweeping valleys of untouched powder,

OPPOSITE: Riding towards the Treriksrøysa (Three-Country Cairn) between Norway, Sweden, and Finland. Each country has its own hut network, which can be nicely linked.

granite outcrops that catch the golden arctic light, and a silence so deep it feels like a form of music.

Yet for all its remoteness, Gappohytta is profoundly communal. It is part of the self-service hut network—a system built on trust, effort, and shared responsibility. Here, skiers stack wood for the next traveler, melt snow for water, and leave a logbook note that becomes part of a long, quiet dialogue between strangers. This unspoken cama-raderie is the soul of the place, offering warmth and comfort deep in a wilderness that offers remark-able beauty in its desolation.

On clear nights, the northern lights often arc overhead in electric silence, dancing across a sky so wide that it seems to swallow the world. Inside the hut, a lantern flickers, boots dry by the stove, and sto-ries are shared over steaming mugs. Not only does Gappohytta represent a coming together on the map but in real life, too. It is a testament to endurance, solitude, and the deep, wordless kinship forged in this arctic far north.

RIGHT: The traditional wood-burning stove, ample wood supply, and large snow-melting pot make keeping warm and preparing water very easy.

SKÅPET

A hamlet of minimalist warmth in the Lysefjord wilderness

LOCATION
FORSAND, NORWAY

COORDINATES
58.986734, 6.342053

ALTITUDE
618 M (2,028 FT)

ACCESS
1.5 HOURS

ACCESSIBILITY
YEAR-ROUND

TYPE
CABINS

SLEEPS
42+ PEOPLE

POINT OF INTEREST
LYSEFJORDEN RUNDT

Tucked into a high, wind-scoured valley above the fjord village of Lysebotn, Skåpet sits like a quiet constellation of shelters in the Ryfylkeheiane mountains of southwestern Norway. Here, where the land sheds its softness and rises into granite, where the clouds seem to skim just overhead, Skåpet offers both refuge and an opportunity for reflection—a place to be held by the landscape, not to conquer it.

The cabins appear suddenly as you crest the final ridge: sharp-edged silhouettes huddled together beneath wide skies and ever-shifting weather. They are built low to the ground, with steeply pitched roofs to shrug off snow and rain, and clad in untreated wood that grays gently with time, allowing them to blend into their surroundings like cairns. The largest cabin stands at the center, its broad glass facade catching the light from the valley and sending it flickering across the smooth wooden walls. This is the hearth of Skåpet—a communal kitchen, a place to eat and rest, where the crackle of the stove and the murmur of shared stories offer comfort against the damp chill outside.

Around it, six smaller cabins stretch along the slope, each angled for privacy and perspective. These sleeping cabins are minimalist yet profoundly comforting: a few bunks, thick wool blankets, and views of the surrounding nature framed like paintings. Their interiors are clean-lined and spare, with pale wood panels and small windows that let in the northern light but keep the cold at bay. The beds are tucked into alcoves like cocoons—places to rest and listen to the wind run its fingers across the roof. With the option of booking an individual cabin, Skåpet offers a unique balance between privacy and the coming together of shared adventure in the communal main cabin.

Further off, almost hidden among the rocks, a sauna cabin sits beside a clear stream that rushes cold and fast through the valley floor. In the stillness of a snowbound evening, its warm interior glows like an ember in the dusk, offering tired limbs and chilled skin a deep, restorative heat that reaches into the bones. There is minimal solar electricity here, no tap water, and no network signal. And yet, everything essential is provided: heat, shelter, and the serenity of solitude. Skåpet feels both ancient and new. Its geometry speaks of modern design, but its purpose is timeless. It's an

answer to the primal question: where will I be safe from the storm?

From the huts, the land opens in all directions. Summer trails wind through birch and boulder, past tarns so still that they mirror the sky. Skåpet lies on the Lysefjorden Rundt, one of Norway's most popular multiday trails. Spanning 100 kilometers (6.8 miles), this scenic trail repeatedly meanders from fjord to mountain. In winter, the journey to the cabins becomes a ski tour—11 kilometers through steep forest and exposed moor, demanding both fitness and focus. Reaching Skåpet under snow is an arrival earned. There is a silence here that speaks louder than words.

Evening drapes itself slowly across the valley. A shared meal, a scribbled journal, the soft curl of spruce smoke rising into the midnight. Skåpet doesn't resist the wilderness—it leans into it. These quiet cabins place you not above nature but cradled within it. More than a waypoint, Skåpet is a rhythm, a retreat, a gentle reminder that at its simplest, life asks only for warmth, stillness, and sky.

OPPOSITE: The individual sleeping cabins feature wonderful modern interiors with views of the nearby Soddatjørna Lake.

RABOTHYTTA

A flagship hut deep in the wild north of Norway with quintessential Scandinavian charm

LOCATION
HELGELAND, NORWAY

COORDINATES
66.006335, 14.139702

ALTITUDE
1,182 M (3,878 FT)

ACCESS
2–4 HOURS

ACCESSIBILITY
YEAR-ROUND

TYPE
BIVOUAC

SLEEPS
30 PEOPLE

POINTS OF INTEREST
OKSTINDBREEN GLACIER
OKSSKOLTEN (1,916 M / 6,286 FT)

High on the weather-hewn shoulders of Okstindan, Norway's oldest mountains, Rabothytta stands like a sentinel against the endless northern sky. At 1,182 m (3,878 ft) above sea level, this striking hut is less a building and more a living testament to the spirit of exploration and endurance that the Helgeland mountains demand. Clad in Siberian larch, its sharp, angular form seems to grow out of the rock and ice around it, a geometric echo of the jagged summits it faces.

Opened in 2014, Rabothytta is the jewel of the Norwegian Trekking Association's (DNT) network in Helgeland, a bold and beautiful refuge named after Charles Rabot, the French explorer who first brought the region's wonders to the wider world in the late 19th century. Rabot was an early pioneer of alpinism and the first to climb Kebnekaise, Sweden's highest mountain. The hut was designed by the renowned Jarmund/Vigsnæs Arkitekter, whose vision was to craft a shelter that could withstand the fury of winter storms while capturing the breathtaking drama of the surrounding landscape. Inside, the warm birch-paneled interior feels both minimalist and yet inviting, a modern embrace after the long and often arduous ascent.

Outside the heavy steel door, a kingdom of glaciers, stone, and sky unfurls. The mighty Okstindbreen Glacier, the largest in mainland Norway, lies just beyond, its ancient mass sighing and creaking in the cold. Towering above, Oksskolten, the highest peak in Northern Norway at 1,916 m (6,286 ft), beckons climbers and ski tourers alike with its proud silhouette. From Rabothytta's panoramic windows, the view is a moving masterpiece of shifting light, mist, and mountain—a spectacle that changes by the hour and humbles all who bear witness. On clear days, you can see all the way to the Helgeland coast.

In winter, Rabothytta becomes a haven for ski mountaineers navigating the high plateaus and glacier routes of Okstindan. In summer, it serves trekkers tracing old reindeer migration paths and ancient Sami routes that weave through the stones. It is not an easy refuge to reach. A steep, rocky path climbs from Leirskardalen Valley, demanding sure footing and a spirit tuned to the mountain's rhythms. But every step is repaid a hundredfold when the hut's sharp silhouette finally appears through the mist and wind.

ABOVE: Rabothytta boasts a sleek design of wood and glass with panoramic views of the glaciers and peaks in the Okstindan range.

Beyond its impressive architectural bravado, Rabothytta pulses with human spirit. Built with the hands and hearts of hundreds of volunteers from the Hemnes chapter of the DNT, its very walls are a symbol of community devotion. Each beam and panel was hauled and hammered into place through collective effort, a true labor of love that mirrors the hut's namesake's passion for this wild frontier. The cabin's interior features six bedrooms, a loft, and a purpose-built room for dogs—a rarity in remote alpine shelters. The cozy common area fosters shared stories over freeze-dried meals and steaming cups of brew, where the fierce solitude of the mountains gives way to the quiet communion of kindred souls.

To spend a night at Rabothytta is to feel, if only briefly, that you're at the edge of the world. Here, amid the hiss of snow against wood, the deep silence of glaciers, and the timeless dance of northern light across blackened sky, one touches something elemental—something enduring and rare. Rabothytta is more than a place to rest: it is a vessel of belonging, carved into Norway's untamed north.

OPPOSITE: The lesser-trodden wilderness around Rabothytta blends pristine Arctic tundra with dramatic, jagged alpine peaks—raw, remote and beautifully humbling.

HOSPICE DU GRAND-SAINT-BERNARD

A grand monastery open to all, with a long-standing and rich history

LOCATION
BOURG-SAINT-PIERRE, SWITZERLAND

COORDINATES
45.869001, 7.170631

ALTITUDE
2,473 M (8,114 FT)

ACCESS
2–3 HOURS (WINTER)

ACCESSIBILITY
YEAR-ROUND

TYPE
REFUGE

SLEEPS
132 PEOPLE

POINTS OF INTEREST
**MONT MORT (2,867 M / 9,406 FT)
GRANDE CHENALETTE (2,890 M / 942 FT)**

This truly unique refuge stands on one of the highest and most beautiful passes dividing Italy and Switzerland. For the summer months, it can be accessed effortlessly by road. However, for almost half of the year, the hospice is cut off from the outside world, standing resolute as a beacon of self-reliance. Snow-buried and lashed by storms that have tested travelers for almost 10 centuries, this ancient refuge acts as a keeper of history and a guardian of the High Alps.

The hospice is a monastic structure with thick stone walls that stand tall against the elements, yet within them pulses a warmth that has saved lives for a millennium. Founded in 1050 by Saint Bernard of Menthon, the patron saint of mountaineers, it was conceived as a resting place and sanctuary of salvation amidst the harsh indifference of snowy mountains, rock, and ice.

To this day, the hospice is run by Augustinian monks, their presence a rare thread of continuity in a world that shifts with every passing season. The corridors of the hospice are lined with heavy wooden doors, each leading to simple yet welcoming rooms where travelers can find respite from the high-altitude cold. The communal dining hall, presumably once filled with flickering candlelight and the glow of a wood-burning stove, now has a more modern feel. Where countless pilgrims once sought solace and sustenance, today, weary skiers and mountaineers gather in quiet camaraderie, bound by the same timeless need for food and warmth. The chapel continues to bear witness to the whispers of three prayer sessions a day, open to everyone but optional for those less inclined.

The Grand-Saint-Bernard Pass has long been a threshold between worlds, a conduit through the Alps connecting Switzerland and Italy. It has seen Roman legions marching toward conquest, Napoleon's army traipsing through snowdrifts, and generations of traders, pilgrims, and mountaineers drawn to its heights. A plaque on the hospice wall commemorates the passing of Napoleon's forces in May 1800, when 46,000 soldiers struggled through the pass in a daring maneuver during the Italian Campaign. Even now, in the age of modern maps and GPS, the hospice remains an indispensable waypoint for those venturing into the remote mountains between Valais and Aosta.

OPPOSITE: Two hikers make their way over the frozen Lac du Grand-Saint-Bernard, crossing into Italy with Grand Golliat (3,238 m) in the distance.

For ski tourers, it is a gateway to an unspoiled winter realm, a place barely touched by the commercialization of ski tourism. The ascent to the hospice itself is a rite of passage, albeit not a technical climb but a slow tour through a narrowing valley where the wind whips through, sculpting snowdrifts as it passes. Arriving at the Hospice du Grand-Saint-Bernard, the stone archway links two different sides of the building, acting as a physical and figurative gateway to an alpine playground. The snow-covered plateau around the hospice, with its sweeping views of the Mont Blanc massif and the Grand Combin, offers a stark beauty that is both intimidating and exhilarating. The nearby Col Ouest de Barasson presents a favored descent for ski tourers, its broad slopes promising long, fluid turns in untouched powder.

In the summer months, once the pass breathes free of its icy grip, hikers and cyclists take up the mantle of the pilgrims before them—tracing ancient paths once trod by mule caravans and contraband smugglers. The air here is thick with history; the Via Francigena, the medieval pilgrimage route that once connected Canterbury to Rome, passes through the hospice. Even today, modern pilgrims retrace its steps, their journey punctuated by the rhythmic chime of cowbells from the alpine pastures below.

Perhaps the most famous residents of the hospice were its legendary St. Bernard dogs, bred for their strength, resilience, and ability to rescue stranded travelers. The hospice's archives hold records of the dogs' heroic feats, including Barry, the most celebrated of them all, who is credited with saving over 40 lives in the early 19th century. Though modern rescue operations no longer rely on them, their legacy continues, and visitors can still meet these gentle giants at the Barry Foundation in the nearby town of Martigny.

Although the Hospice du Grand-Saint-Bernard was built to support travelers' long journeys, it has evolved into a destination in and of itself. Traversing the snowy expanse to reach the hut, your journey into the wild feels as though it transcends time, and in a world that moves faster and faster, it remains a sanctuary of calm for all who seek it.

ABOVE: Inside, a fascinating tour through history is a testament to the long-standing tradition of offering passersby refuge.
OPPOSITE: Nathan Hughes enjoying some cold snow skiing down to the hut.

HOSPICE DU GRAND-SAINT-BERNARD

JUBILÄUMSGRATHÜTTE

A simple red shelter perched in the heart of one of the most iconic ridge traverses in the Alps

LOCATION
GARMISCH-PARTENKIRCHEN, GERMANY

COORDINATES
47.420870, 11.026353

ALTITUDE
2,684 M (8,806 FT)

ACCESS
3–4 HOURS

ACCESSIBILITY
YEAR-ROUND

TYPE
BIVOUAC

SLEEPS
12 PEOPLE

POINTS OF INTEREST
JUBILÄUMSGRAT
ZUGSPITZE (2,962 M / 9,718 FT)
HOCHBLASSEN (2,706 M / 8,878 FT)

Clinging to a narrow col along one of the most formidable ridgelines in the Eastern Alps, the Jubiläumsgrathütte is less a hut and more a lifeline—an angular steel bivouac box welded into the very bones of the mountain. At 2,684 m (8,806 ft) above sea level, suspended between the lofty crests of the Zugspitze and the Alpspitze, it offers little comfort, no warmth, and no host. And yet, in the harsh clarity of high alpine terrain, it represents something profound: survival, pause, and the thin threshold between endurance and retreat.

The shelter is simple and small—just enough for 12 people to lie shoulder to shoulder in two bunks of three close-knit sleeping spaces on each side. Inside, it is austere: compact mattresses lined up with a few blankets and emergency supplies. But it is dry, solid, still. When storms scream across the ridge and clouds swallow the peaks, this unmanned box becomes a sacred reprieve. To arrive here is to feel the tension ease from your shoulders, your heartbeat finally slow, your senses return. For the exhausted climber on the Jubiläumsgrat, it is not luxury, but salvation.

The Jubiläumsgrat—or "Anniversary Ridge"—is an uncompromising traverse that stretches for nearly 5 km (3 mi) between the Zugspitze (2,962 m / 9,718 ft), Germany's highest peak, and the sharply pyramidal Alpspitze (2,628 m / 8,622 ft). First climbed in 1897 and already named in 1894 to commemorate the 25th anniversary of the Munich section of the German Alpine Club, this absolute classic alpine route is a magnificent study in exposure and commitment. Knife-edge ridges, plunging chimneys, and jagged pinnacles demand not only technical skill but also mental stamina. The rock is Wetterstein limestone—sharp, solid, and unforgiving.

Roughly midway along this ridge, the Jubiläumsgrathütte offers the only fixed shelter. Originally built in 1962, it was replaced in the summer of 2011: its 90th. Its presence allows climbers to break the route into two long days and has saved countless lives in the event of fatigue, injury, or frequently changing weather. It represents the serious, uncompromising spirit of alpine climbing: purposeful, self-reliant, elemental.

To the west rises the Zugspitze, a mountain with a split identity. On one face, a highly developed popular summit with restaurants, viewing platforms, and cable cars humming up from the valleys. On the other,

a wilderness of snowfields, ice, and rock. The Jubiläumsgrat begins just beyond the handrails and warning signs—a line that separates commercial tourism from true alpine commitment. While not far from the hustle and bustle of the Zugspitze cable car, it offers brave visitors a true alpine experience as if they were deep in the silence of untouched wilderness.

In good weather, the views from the hut are searingly beautiful: the crumpled ranges of the Wetterstein spreading outward, the depths of the Höllental yawning beneath, and the pale spires of the Alpspitze rising to the east. When the weather turns stormy, the world contracts to the cold metal walls and the breath of those beside you.

There is a quiet nobility to the Jubiläumsgrathütte. It does not ask to be admired, only respected. It reminds us that not all refuges are soft places. Some, like this one, are forged in steel and solitude, made to stand where few can—enduring the storm so that those who dare may find, however briefly, a place to rest.

OPPOSITE: The Jubiläumsgrat is an iconic alpine ridge traverse between Zugspitze and Alpspitze, on which this bivouac is strategically positioned.

REFUGE DE L'AIGLE

A historic and compact refuge perched on the edge of the coveted Massif des Écrins

LOCATION
ÉCRINS NATIONAL PARK, FRANCE

COORDINATES
45.011213, 6.324563

ALTITUDE
3,450 M (11,319 FT)

ACCESS
6 HOURS

ACCESSIBILITY
APRIL–MAY & JUNE–AUGUST

TYPE
REFUGE

SLEEPS
30 PEOPLE

POINTS OF INTEREST
LA MEIJE (3,984 M / 13,071 FT)
BEC DE L'HOMME (3,454 M / 11,332 FT)

Perched like a weathered eagle clinging to a rocky aerie, the Refuge de l'Aigle defies gravity and convention at 3,450 m (11,319 ft) above sea level. Anchored to a narrow granite ridge of the Massif des Écrins, it gazes solemnly across the high flanks of La Meije, the crown jewel of the Southern French Alps. This is not a refuge one stumbles upon, high above the valley. It is only earned with sweat, altitude, and reverence.

To reach the Refuge de l'Aigle is to ascend through worlds. The route begins near the iconic mountain village of La Grave, that storied place where time knots itself into avalanches of history and ice. From the alpine meadows, climbers ascend past tumbling seracs and the bleached skeletons of moraine. As altitude bites, civilization recedes below, replaced by a stark, immediate clarity where every step demands focus, and every sound feels distant. Then, from a final scramble of shattered rock, the hut appears—unbelievably small, astonishingly brave.

The current refuge is a reconstruction—completed in 2014—of the original 1910 structure that stood for over a century. The rebuild, led with sensitivity and restraint, preserves the spartan soul of the original while strengthening its bones for a new era of storms. With its wood paneling, sleek profile, and metallic sheen sidewalls, it evokes both a mountain chapel and a lunar lander—an icon of alpine minimalism. Inside, it sleeps around 30, comparatively small for a manned refuge, with narrow bunks, warm wood panels, and panoramic windows that frame the Meije's untamed face. There is no running water, no luxury, no noise—only the gentle clinking of tea mugs and the wind outside, moving like memory through stone.

Historically, the refuge has served as the gateway to some of the most storied ascents in the Alps. From here, alpinists step into a cathedral of granite and ice. The Traverse of La Meije—a legendary route that flows across jagged ridges and steep snowfields—is often staged from the Refuge de l'Aigle. In winter, the hut transforms into a beacon for ski mountaineers tracing the high lines of the Écrins. Despite not being accessed by the resort-lift network, reaching it in deep snow with skins or crampons remains a rite of passage for those drawn to the raw verticality of the La Grave.

But beyond its strategic role, the shelter holds something deeper. It represents a kind of pilgrimage—a journey to a high place where human fragility meets the enduring strength of stone. And when dusk falls and the alpenglow sets La Meije ablaze in rose and gold, the refuge stands quietly, bearing witness to courage, to solitude, to the enduring pull of high places. A century of climbers have shared experiences in this wild massif, shared cups of broth after a night spent battling wind and doubt. Here in this compact but beautiful refuge, high above the clouds, camaraderie becomes elemental. Above it all, the sky feels boundless, and the mountain, indifferent. In the stillness, there is a clarity that comes only from distance—both from the valley below and from the noise of the world. Here, in this silence, the weight of the journey settles in, and with it, a quiet understanding.

ABOVE: From the refuge, the views are almost 360 degrees, offering a fantastic observation point over the jagged peaks of Pointe Nérot (3,537 m), Pointe des Pichettes (3,534 m), and many more.

RIGHT: The interior is bright, spacious, and well-designed, with the sleeping nooks tucked behind colorful curtains next to the high-ceilinged living space.

REFUGE DE L'AIGLE

BERGGASTHAUS AESCHER

A fairytale mountain refuge that blends legend and landscape in the wild heart of Appenzell

LOCATION
WEISSBAD, SWITZERLAND

COORDINATES
47.283400, 9.414393

ALTITUDE
1,454 M (4,770 FT)

ACCESS
1–2 HOURS

ACCESSIBILITY
MAY–NOVEMBER

TYPE
REFUGE

SLEEPS
33 PEOPLE

POINTS OF INTEREST
SEEALPSEE LAKE
SÄNTIS (2,502 M / 8,209 FT)

Clinging to the side of a vertical cliff in the Alpstein massif, the Aescher-Gasthaus am Berg is a place that defies expectation and gravity alike. Set beneath the towering limestone face of the Ebenalp at 1,454 m (4,770 ft), this beautifully traditional wooden guesthouse seems to have emerged from the rock itself—less built than discovered. Framed by crag and sky, it has become one of the most iconic mountain refuges in the Alps, not for its altitude or isolation, but for its sheer improbability and picture-postcard Swiss charm.

Reaching the Aescher is a journey that winds through a landscape of storybook beauty and geological drama. Hikers begin their ascent in the Appenzell countryside, where green meadows roll like soft waves and tidy chalets dot the hillsides. The path steepens through spruce forest, fragrant and cool, where the trail is softened by moss and pine needles. Higher still, the route passes through the Wildkirchli caves—ancient limestone caverns once used by hermits and, even earlier, Neanderthals. Stepping out from these shadowed chambers into the light, the hut appears suddenly, impossibly, clinging to the cliff like a secret kept by the mountain.

The Berggasthaus Aescher has existed in its current form since 1860, making it one of the oldest mountain huts in Switzerland, but the history of hermits living deep in these cliffs goes back two centuries further. Since then, this mystical place has fascinated generations—stories abound of little wild people who once lived in the Wildkirchli caves, serving simple fare to local shepherds and wandering pilgrims. Over time, it became a resting place for climbers, hikers, and lovers of alpine solitude. Though small and rustic with wood-paneled walls, creaking floors, a handful of rooms, and communal tables, it offers something few places can: a seat at the edge of the world. Here, guests sip coffee or beer beneath a sheer stone ceiling, watching clouds drift below and eagles wheel above.

From Aescher, an extensive trail network fans out across the Alpstein range, leading to the summit of Säntis, the region's highest peak. The panorama from its summit is so vast that on clear days, the views extend over six countries: Switzerland, Germany, Austria, Liechtenstein, France, and Italy. The lesser-known ridgelines offer more peace off the beaten track, where ibex

ABOVE: Inside, you'll find a beautiful blend of wood with original stone walls, in keeping with the mythical cave-dwelling history of settlers on these cliffs.

roam and the silence feels ancient. Berggasthaus Aescher is a perfect waypoint for day hikers and multi-day wanderers alike, offering shelter within one of the most geologically rich corners of the Swiss Alps. The surrounding rock is full of folds and fractures, shaped by millennia of uplift and erosion, while the flora—edelweiss, alpine clover, and gentian—clings to ledges and pastures with quiet tenacity.

As with many of Switzerland's gems, the refuge attracts people from all over the world either for food or an overnight stay, but early in the morning or just before dusk, when the people recede, the true atmosphere settles in. The rock breathes. The wind carries the sound of distant cowbells. Light slides down the cliff face, painting it in rose and lavender hues, staining the stone with the hush of evening.

To sit at the edge of Aescher's narrow terrace is to feel the grandeur of the Alps not in isolation but in intimacy. It is a place shaped by time, by labor, and by the enduring human need to seek shelter in the most unlikely of places.

ABOVE: Those not wanting to climb from the bottom can descend on foot from the Ebenalp cable car, making it an accessible hut experience for families.

HANNIBAL BIVOUAC

A gleaming, hidden gem nestled on the border between France and Italy

LOCATION
GIAGLIONE, ITALY

COORDINATES
45.167044, 6.918563

ALTITUDE
2,477 M (8,127 FT)

ACCESS
4–5 HOURS

ACCESSIBILITY
YEAR-ROUND

TYPE
BIVOUAC

SLEEPS
8 PEOPLE

POINTS OF INTEREST
MONT GIUSALET (3,312 M / 10,866 FT)
DENTS D'AMBIN (3,372 M / 11,063 FT)

At the cusp of two worlds, where France and Italy convene in a cold and wind-bitten pass, the Hannibal Bivouac stands as a homage to centuries of human passage. Nestled on a high plateau at Col de Clapier, for which the bivouac also shares another name, this humble-yet-defiant structure is a welcome refuge in an otherwise inhospitable wilderness. Although technically not a long distance from the nearest villages as the crow flies, its dramatic and complex mountain terrain grants a feeling of palpable remoteness.

The bivouac itself is a modest, functional refuge—a simple metal shell reinforced against even the mountain's worst moods. Inside, the space is austere yet welcoming, with wooden bunks and a table where weary hikers and mountaineers can rest their legs and share stories in the flickering glow of headlamps. There is no guardian here, meaning supplies must be carried in—no easy feat in winter, especially from the Italian side, which involves almost 1,500 m (4,921 ft) of steep, unrelenting ascent. There are, however, eight sleeping places with appropriate bedding provisions, solar electricity providing a modest heating system, and a light that shines brightly at night to help those seeking shelter.

The setting is nothing short of spectacular. To the west, the rugged flanks of Mont d'Ambin rise like a frozen fortress, its ridges dusted with snow well into the summer. To the east, the Italian valleys unfurl in a patchwork of rocky ridges and impressive towers, no doubt the remnants of glaciers that have since faded away. Here, the silence is immense, an almost tangible presence only broken by the freely roaming ibex and the distant murmur of unseen streams carving their way down to gentler pastures.

History clings to this pass like frost on the rocks, whispering stories of old trade routes and the ceaseless migration of people and ideas. It is believed that this was the mythical route that esteemed military general Hannibal took when leading his army across the Alps to defeat the Romans in 218 BCE, a feat which gained them strategic control of Southern Italy. The army was forced to cross the Alps because they lacked the allied ports necessary to travel by sea. He and his army of 70,000 men, 20,000 horses, and 37 elephants completed the arduous alpine crossing in only 16 days.

ABOVE: The beautiful wooden interior features a panoramic window overlooking the Vallon de Savine on the French side of the border.

While historians debate the exact location, the name persists—a tribute to one of history's greatest military feats. Following in their footsteps, it's hard to believe and yet somehow easy to imagine thousands of Carthaginian soldiers marching forward, their horses and elephants bewildered by the cruel embrace of mountains. The bivouac that stands today is a modern addition with an ancient spirit that echoes all those who have struggled through this high and inhospitable mountain pass.

Hannibal Bivouac serves as a vital waypoint for mountaineers and ski tourers threading their way through the wild terrain of the Ambin massif. For those who arrive, whether by the sweat of summer ascents or the calculated precision of a winter approach, the bivouac is a reminder of the mountain's paradoxes. It is both brutal and beautiful, unforgiving yet generous. For most, however, the bivouac is much more than just a temporary resting place. It is a remarkable destination that honors the legacy of ancient warriors and modern-day mountaineers.

HANNIBAL BIVOUAC

ABOVE RIGHT: Enjoying the south-facing sunshine and views of the numerous 3,000-m peaks that make up the border, offering plenty of interesting ski objectives.

LALIDERERSPITZEN-BIWAK

A solitary steel bivouac offering stark shelter beneath the Karwendel's limestone walls

LOCATION
TYROL, AUSTRIA

COORDINATES
47.390139, 11.503335

ALTITUDE
2,495 M (8,186 FT)

ACCESS
6–8 HOURS

ACCESSIBILITY
YEAR-ROUND

TYPE
BIVOUAC

SLEEPS
6 PEOPLE

POINTS OF INTEREST
THE LALIDERER WALLS
LALIDERER SPITZE (2,588 M / 8,491 FT)
DREIZINKENSPITZE (2,603 M / 8,540 FT)

Tucked between soaring peaks of the Karwendel's northern citadel, the Lalidererspitzen-Biwak is a structure so discreet and spare that it seems to have grown from the very stone that surrounds it. No flag flaps from its side; no signpost points the way. It reveals itself only to those who have earned the view—alpinists with calves burning from steep scrambles under silhouettes of jagged limestone towers.

Sitting on the remote saddle at almost 2,500 m (8,202 ft), adjacent to the peak that shares its name, the bivouac perches in quiet deference to the mountains it serves. Its form is utilitarian—an austere, reflective metallic shell, bolted to the rock to withstand the Karwendel's scouring winds and sudden storms. Inside, it offers minimalist shelter: wooden bunks, a small table, and walls proudly adorned with alpine-club stickers and route maps. There is no stove, no water, no wood—just six beds, a roof, and the solitude of the high mountains.

There is no straightforward approach to the Laliderer—either a lengthy 20-km (12-mile) hike from Scharnitz, with the option to link up with one of the other nearby huts, or for the brave, climbing the north wall itself. Surrounding it is one of the most solemn and untouched landscapes in the Eastern Alps. The Laliderer walls rise sheer and stern above the bivouac, like ancient ramparts of a forgotten fortress. Below, the Lalider Valley stretches out—a long, forested trench where spruce and beech woods roll down to meadows scattered with wild thyme, gentian, and alpine rose. Chamois pick their way along impossible ledges, and in the stillness, the echo of distant rockfall speaks louder than any birdsong. The bivouac's origins are as modest as its presence. Erected in 1971 by the Innsbruck section of the Austrian Alpine Club, it was originally named the Konrad-Schuster-Biwak after the founder of the club's "Gipfelstürmer" group. Intended not as a destination but as a lifeline, the emergency outpost functions as a base for mountain rescues and is equipped with a telephone that connects directly to Tyrol's emergency assistance services. The bivouac also accommodates climbers tackling the long and committing north faces of the Laliderer Spitze, Dreizinkenspitze, and beyond. Routes like the Herzogkante or the Direkte Nordwand demand early starts and even more of the human spirit. The bivouac offers a rare pause before or after such

OPPOSITE: The Laliderer north wall is an impossibly vertical face, almost 1,000 m tall, which can be climbed by multiple routes in roughly 20 pitches.

undertakings—a place to collect thoughts, wait out the weather, or simply survive the night in relative comfort.

Once rarely visited by hikers, the bivouac has grown in popularity in recent years. As such, the Austrian Alpine Club has stipulated that the hut should be reserved for emergency purposes, especially for those who have climbed the infamous north wall. The bivouac still holds quiet reverence among the climbing community. There is no glamour here, only necessity. It is a place where wet ropes are uncoiled in the dark, where boots are left by the door heavy with mud and snow. Those who rest here often leave behind a note or a page torn from a map—small relics in a high place, part of an unwritten book of effort and endurance.

What makes the Laladererspitzen-Biwak so stirring is not comfort or architecture but placement. It sits on the threshold between wilderness and wall, where the cultivated beauty of the valley gives way to the sublime severity of the peaks. In that liminal space, it stands as a mute companion to those who step beyond the paths and into the vertical. A place of cold nights and hard decisions, and of mountain silence so deep it envelopes the soul.

OPPOSITE: The Lalidererspitzen-Biwak is a wild alpine perch deep in the Karwendel. The area feels incredibly raw and remote despite being close to the bustling city of Innsbruck.

MONTE ROSA HÜTTE

A state-of-the-art flagship refuge granting access to countless 4,000-m peaks in the Monte Rosa massif

LOCATION
ZERMATT, SWITZERLAND

COORDINATES
45.956837, 7.814635

ALTITUDE
2,883 M (9,459 FT)

ACCESS
5–7 HOURS

ACCESSIBILITY
MARCH–MAY & JUNE–SEPTEMBER

TYPE
REFUGE

SLEEPS
120 PEOPLE

POINTS OF INTEREST
DUFOURSPITZE (4,634 M / 15,203 FT)
LYSKAMM (4,532 M / 14,869 FT)
SIGNALKUPPE (4,554 M / 14,941 FT)

High above the Gorner Glacier's restless flow, the Monte Rosa Hütte rises from its granite throne, a gleaming and futuristic refuge set against the vast, untamed wilderness of the highest peaks in the Swiss Alps. It represents the modern aspirations of the Swiss Alpine Club as a flagship of green architecture, operating with 90-percent self-sufficiency. For many visitors, the journey begins at the Gornergrat Railway from the chocolate-box and historic mountain town of Zermatt. Once leaving the train, the trail winds through landscapes of impossible grandeur before descending onto the glacier. From here, climbers and ski mountaineers trace a route through a shifting world of crevasses and snow bridges, where each footstep presents a dialogue with the ice beneath.

The hut is a marvel of modern engineering, an angular, silver-clad beacon designed to stand out yet somehow harmonize with its high-altitude surroundings. Completed in 2009, it stands as one of the most sustainable mountain refuges in the world, powered by solar energy and built with cutting-edge efficiency. Its reflective exterior mirrors the ever-changing light of the mountains, at times blending seamlessly into the landscape, at others standing starkly against the encroaching glaciers. The five-story structure is anchored securely to the granite beneath, its sharply angled surfaces designed to shed heavy snowfall and withstand the harsh alpine climate.

Inside, warm wooden interiors contrast the cold world outside, offering a sanctuary where climbers can shed their frozen layers, gather around communal tables, and watch the light shift over the surrounding peaks. The main dining hall is spacious and bright, with panoramic windows that provide sweeping views of the Matterhorn and the spectacular north face of Lyskamm. Meals are hearty and simple, designed to replenish exhausted mountaineers before and after their ascents. The hut can accommodate up to 120 guests in its dormitory-style sleeping quarters, which feature wooden bunk beds with thick blankets.

Modern yet minimal, all the hut's facilities were designed with efficiency and sustainability in mind. A state-of-the-art water purification system collects and filters meltwater from the glacier, while photovoltaic panels generate electricity to power lighting and essential

systems. Despite its remote location, the hut maintains a well-equipped kitchen, a drying room for damp gear, warm showers at a modest cost, and even limited Wi-Fi access. A small library of mountaineering literature offers inspiration for future climbs, while maps and weather reports are posted daily, fueling discussion of endless possible adventures.

The Monte Rosa Hütte is a gateway to countless 4,000-m (13,123-ft) peaks and some of the most coveted climbs and ski traverses in the Alps. It serves as a base for ascents of the Dufourspitze, Switzerland's highest peak at 4,634 m (15,203 ft), as well as numerous other summits in the Monte Rosa massif. In spring, ski tourers set out from its doors to traverse the vast glacial expanses, linking high mountain passes in journeys that test both skill and endurance. For those looking for a multiday adventure in the mountains, the Monte Rosa Hütte can be linked neatly with the refuges on the Italian side of the massif, including the Capanna Gnifetti and Margherita Hut. The route to the hut itself is often an adventure, requiring careful navigation through glacial terrain, where the crevasses shift with the seasons, and safe passage is never guaranteed. When snow conditions are favorable, it's possible to ski down to Zermatt, although late in spring, the meltwater may be too deep to navigate, forcing skiers to go around the glaciated valley.

Despite the unapologetic modernity of the refuge today, its history stretches back to 1895, when the first Monte Rosa hut was built to serve early alpinists drawn to the massif's formidable summits. That original stone structure stood for over a century, witnessing generations of climbers setting out into the unforgiving mountains above, a constant that remains to this day.

As night falls, the world beyond the hut fades into darkness, the glacier glowing faintly under the stars. The silence is profound, broken only by the occasional crack of shifting ice. Inside, a quiet camaraderie settles among those preparing mentally and physically for the next day's ascent, where the thin air will challenge all those brave enough to scale the surrounding high summits.

OPPOSITE: Soaking in the sun on the large wooden terrace overlooking the Grenz Glacier and numerous 4,000-m peaks.

ABOVE: The hut is a staging post for numerous ski and alpinism objectives, most notably Dufourspitze (4,634 m), the second-highest peak in the Alps.

CAPANNA REGINA MARGHERITA

The highest refuge in Europe with over a century of fascinating history

LOCATION
VERCELLI, ITALY

COORDINATES
45.926963, 7.877106

ALTITUDE
4,554 M (14,941 FT)

ACCESS
1–2 DAYS

ACCESSIBILITY
JUNE–SEPTEMBER

TYPE
REFUGE

SLEEPS
70 PEOPLE

POINTS OF INTEREST
SIGNALKUPPE (4,554 M / 14,941 FT)
DUFOURSPITZE (4,634 M / 15,203 FT)
ZUMSTEINSPITZE (4,563 M / 14,970 FT)

Built on the summit of one of the highest peaks in the Alps, Capanna Regina Margherita is the highest mountain refuge in Europe, a mark of early human resilience clinging to the icy shoulder of Signalkuppe (Punta Gnifetti) high in the Monte Rosa massif. Here, where the air is thin and the world below blurs into a dreamscape of glaciers and craggy ridgelines, the hut stands as both a beacon of shelter and a testament to alpine ambition.

To arrive at the Capanna Regina Margherita is to embark on a journey that is as much about endurance as it is about arrival. The most common ascent begins from Alagna Valsesia or Gressoney, following a chain of lower refuges including Gnifetti or Mantova—before climbers make their final push across the glacier, roped together against the ever-present risks of crevasses and the firm grip of altitude. The last steps to the hut are an act of will, each crampon crunching into snow that has known no summer, the wind often howling its ancient song against the ridge.

And then, there it is: a wooden hut seemingly grafted onto the rock, its dark metal and wood facade contrasting sharply against the cobalt sky. The hut itself is an ever-impressive feat of engineering, anchored into the mountain by the Italian Alpine Club in 1893. The original hut was prefabricated in the valley before being carried to the peak by mules and men and assembled on-site. In a rare feat for royalty of the era, Queen Margherita of Savoy, who was Queen of Italy, climbed to the summit of Signalkuppe to personally open the hut in the company of prominent alpinists, guides, politicians, and aristocrats. The refuge soon became an important research outpost for high-altitude medicine, and a meteorological station was also added, recording temperatures as low as −37.5 °C (−35.5 °F). Despite its extremely isolated perch, it has evolved into a sophisticated outpost over the decades, equipped with dormitories and an impressively well-equipped kitchen.

Inside, it's easy to forget you're drinking hot tea on one of the highest peaks in the Alps. However, at these dizzying heights, even acclimatized mountaineers can expect a night of broken sleep as the body works hard to compensate for the lack of oxygen. The wooden interior, simple yet sturdy, offers a rare comfort in this realm of ice and silence. Climbers huddle around steaming mugs, their faces flushed from exertion and

exposure, recounting their ascent or planning the next day's route. Here, stories are a shared bond forged in altitude and effort.

The hut is a gateway to the numerous 4,000-m (13,123-ft) summits of Monte Rosa. From its doorstep, alpinists set forth towards Signalkuppe, Zumsteinspitze, and even the Dufourspitze, the highest point in Switzerland—via the normal Italian route. In winter, when the mountains drape themselves in even deeper solitude, ski mountaineers chart their paths through great white expanses, many attempting some variant of the "Spaghetti tour," a classic high-altitude route traversing the massif.

To sleep in the Capanna Regina Margherita is to drift in the rarefied realm of mountaineering pioneers. At night, the altitude whispers in your veins, sleep comes in fractured dreams, and the wind presses against the walls, a reminder that even here, nature holds dominion. But come dawn, when the first light ignites the peaks in orange and rose hues, there is a moment—fleeting, perfect—when the world feels infinite, and the mountains seem to breathe with you.

ABOVE RIGHT: Directly off the terrace, the exposure is humbling. **NEXT PAGE:** Tom Grant skiing the Marinelli Couloir—one of the longest ski descents in the world.

ABOVE: The hut's wood-paneled bedrooms are simple and cozy with bunk beds, pillows, and thick wool blankets.

RAMOLHAUS

A traditional stone sanctuary offering panoramic views over the Ötztal Alps

LOCATION
TYROL, AUSTRIA

COORDINATES
46.829519, 10.969653

ALTITUDE
3,006 M (8,962 FT)

ACCESS
3–4 HOURS

ACCESSIBILITY
JUNE–SEPTEMBER

TYPE
REFUGE

SLEEPS
52 PEOPLE

POINTS OF INTEREST
**GROSSER RAMOLKOGEL (3,549 M / 11,644 FT)
FIRMISANSCHNEIDE (3,491 M / 11,453 FT)
SCHALFKOGEL (3,537 M / 11,604 FT)**

Reaching the starting point, the peaceful mountain resort of Obergurgl feels like a journey in and of itself, especially for those coming from Italian Tyrol over the ever-impressive Timmelsjoch Pass. The enormity of the mountainscape here is never-ending. Encircled by glaciers and jagged peaks, the village itself clings to the edge of wilderness, where the road ends and the true mountains begin.

From there, the approach on foot begins gently enough, through larch and pine forests that thin with altitude, their needles whispering with alpine wind. Marmots skitter across rocky slopes, and the calls of choughs spiral down from unseen heights. As you rise, the valley narrows, and the path twists between moraine and wildflower-dappled meadows. Even in summer, patches of persistent snow cling to the hollows, and the air grows sharper and cleaner, thinned of lowland distractions.

At over 3,000 m (9,843 ft) above sea level, Ramolhaus is perched like an eagle's aerie above the Gurglertal Valley, keeping vigil over a wilder world carved by ice and wind. This stone refuge, built in 1881 by mountain guide Martinus Scheiber, is anchored into the rocky buttress as if it has always belonged, the slate-gray and steel-blue hues broken only by its defiantly bright red shutters. The hut is one of the highest in the Tyrol, a granite beacon between sky and snow, where the realm of men begins to blur into the dominion of Austria's most expansive glaciers.

Ramolhaus rises unexpectedly at the end of this long ascent, tucked against the Ramolkamm ridge like a fortress hewn from the mountains. From its terraces, the panorama is staggering: the jagged silhouettes of the Schnalskamm range to the west, the blue-white bulk of the Gurgler Ferner Glacier spilling below, and, to the south, the ice-silvered summits of Similaun and Hintere Schwärze. The hut gazes directly into the raw heart of the Eastern Alps.

Despite its altitude, Ramolhaus feels less austere than one might expect. Inside, the thick stone walls enclose rooms washed in warm light, wood-framed and lovingly worn by decades of mountaineers. There is a quiet pride here, a continuity of purpose passed from warden to warden. Meals are hearty, the stove warm, and conversations blend languages and generations.

ABOVE: The view from Ramolhaus spans the upper Ötztal Alps, with clear sightlines to peaks like Ramolkogel and Spiegelkogel.

Historically, Ramolhaus was a keystone in the golden age of alpinism. Scheiber's vision was clear: to create a base for ascents of Wildspitze (3,768 m/12,362 ft), the highest peak in Tyrol, and to open the remote southern flanks of the Ötztal for exploration. From the hut, one can reach the Ramolkogel, Spiegelkogel, the Schalfkogel, or even the Similaun—routes that echo with the footsteps of early pioneers and modern alpinists alike.

In more recent times, the Ramolhaus has undergone sensitive renovations, balancing heritage with sustainability. Rainwater harvesting, solar energy, and thoughtful architecture preserve the hut's essential ruggedness while reducing its environmental footprint. And though the access remains demanding, this remoteness is part of its essence, filtering the hurried from the devoted.

This is where clouds can sweep in like curtains drawn across the sky, dawn casts golden fire on the glacier's ribs, and solitude takes on a rare, crystalline clarity. The Ramolhaus provides relative comfort, practically, and on a deeper level, offering a sense of clarity, belonging, and profound stillness that can only be found while overlooking these vast glacial vistas.

OPPOSITE: The balcony trail to reach the hut is varied, taking you from rich alpine meadows to rocky, jagged, and snowbound peaks.

STÜDLHÜTTE

A sturdy refuge nestled beneath the soaring flanks of Austria's highest peak

LOCATION
HOHE TAUERN NATIONAL PARK, AUSTRIA

COORDINATES
47.054884, 12.681116

ALTITUDE
2,801 M (9,190 FT)

ACCESS
2–3 HOURS

ACCESSIBILITY
MARCH–MAY & JUNE–SEPTEMBER

TYPE
REFUGE

SLEEPS
100 PEOPLE

POINTS OF INTEREST
GROSSGLOCKNER (3,798 M / 12,461 FT)
ROMARISWANDKÖPFE (3,508 M / 11,509 FT)

Sitting at the edge of a glacial amphitheater beneath the brooding shadow of the Großglockner, Austria's highest mountain, the Stüdlhütte stands like a sentinel of metal and wood—weathered, wise, and unyielding. Here, above the line where larch forests soon give way to scree and snow, the air thins, and the silence deepens, broken only by the whisper of wind across rock and the distant groan of glacial movement. The hut itself is a study in alpine resilience and quiet beauty. Rebuilt in 1996 to meet modern needs while honoring its heritage, the current structure seamlessly blends steel and wood with sweeping glass panels that offer stirring views across the Ködnitz Valley and up toward the serrated ridgeline of the Stüdlgrat. Solar panels gleam on the roof, a nod to sustainability at high altitude, and inside, the warmth of stone walls and polished wood creates a welcoming contrast to the world of ice just beyond the threshold.

Stüdlhütte is a high-alpine crossroad, a place where dreams of ascent and the realities of altitude intertwine. For many, it is the final staging ground before tackling the Großglockner, whether by the technically demanding Stüdlgrat, the classic Glocknerleitl, or in winter, by ski over the glacier-cloaked flanks. The hut becomes a crucible in the dark hours before dawn, when climbers rise into the chill to tie their knots, shoulder their packs, and step into the white unknown. In this moment, camaraderie transcends language: a nod and a shared silence.

The history of the hut reaches back to the vision of Johann Stüdl, a Bohemian merchant and mountaineer who, in the mid-19th century, championed the construction of safe paths and refuges in the Eastern Alps. His legacy lives not just in the hut's name but in the very path that bears his ambition—the Stüdlgrat, an elegant, airy ridge-route first climbed in 1864, which still ranks among the most beautiful climbs in the Eastern Alps. The original Stüdlhütte was one of the oldest in Tyrol, a humble wooden structure built in 1868. Over the years, it evolved, was knocked down, rebuilt, and finally reimagined into the eco-conscious refuge that welcomes today's generation of alpinists.

Inside the Stüdlhütte, the mood shifts from glacial austerity to the warm, communal heartbeat of a mountain refuge crafted and maintained with care. The hut blends wood, stone, and steel into a welcoming alpine

OPPOSITE: The hut sits under the watchful eye of Fanatkogel (2,905 m) and features numerous environmentally conscious features, including solar panels and biological wastewater treatment.

interior. The main dining room features wooden walls glowing golden in lamplight and long, bench-lined communal tables worn smooth by decades of elbows. Large windows frame the glacial world outside, but the hut's heart is its stove, radiating quiet warmth even as storms howl beyond the walls.

In winter, the hut becomes a beacon for ski tourers tracing graceful arcs through the Glockner group. Routes radiate like frozen tributaries from its doors: to the summit of Romariswandköpfe, over the Teischnitzkees Glacier, or across to the Adlersruhe. When dusk falls, the blue hour swallows the valleys below, and the hut glows golden against the snow—its common room filled with laughter, local Glöckner wine, and maps spread wide over worn wooden tables.

Stüdlhütte is not merely a waypoint; it is part of the mountain itself—rooted in stone, steeped in history, and alive with the quiet pulse of those who pass through it. To spend a night here is to take your place in a long procession of seekers, drawn upward by a shared longing for height, solitude, and the summit of Austria's grandest massif.

ABOVE: Paul Lange navigating the summit ridge towards the Großglockner, Austria's highest peak. **NEXT PAGE:** Four skiers make their final approach to the hut, a great base for spring ski touring.

REFUGE DE PRESSET

A modern outpost of warmth and wood, nestled beneath the legendary Pierra Menta

LOCATION
BEAUFORTAIN, FRANCE

COORDINATES
45.648256, 6.663775

ALTITUDE
2,514 M (8,248 FT)

ACCESS
2–4 HOURS

ACCESSIBILITY
FEBRUARY–APRIL & JUNE–SEPTEMBER

TYPE
REFUGE

SLEEPS
30 PEOPLE

POINTS OF INTEREST
**PIERRA MENTA (2,714 M / 8,904 FT)
AIGUILLE DU GRAND FOND (2,920 M / 9,580 FT)
TOUR DU BEAUFORTAIN**

Refuge de Presset is a modern and welcoming refuge nestled in the quiet, untamed reaches of the Beaufortain massif—an often-overlooked corner of the Alps that lies between the towering presence of Mont Blanc and the resorts of the Tarentaise Valley. It sits like a quiet sentinel beside its namesake lake. In early summer, the final remnants of winter's blanket melt away, revealing a dark, glacial tarn that reflects the jagged ridgeline of the Pierra Menta with near-mythical clarity.

The refuge, while striking, does not dominate the skyline. Its sleek profile and contemporary wood-and-metal structure are designed to harmonize with the surrounding landscape, evoking the clean lines and natural materials of a Scandinavian cabin rather than the rustic aesthetic one might associate with a traditional alpine refuge. The large south-facing windows pull in the changing moods of the sky, and inside, the atmosphere is warm and communal. The long wooden tables and benches for all guests deliver a banquet-like atmosphere, complemented by three courses of tasty, locally produced food. In the winter, the stove crackles, drawing guests together to tell their stories. Managed with a quiet diligence, the refuge upholds the traditions of mountain hospitality, where a bowl of soup and a welcoming nod can be as restorative as a warm bed. Sleeping areas are divided into dormitories of six, a welcome division for those more susceptible to loud sleepers, and beds are positioned high for additional personal space.

The surrounding terrain showcases a stunning alpine transition. Below, the lower valleys are stitched with pine forests and alpine meadows, where marmots whistle, and the scent of wild thyme mingles with moss. As one climbs higher from the Cormet de Roselend or Arêches, the trees give way to rock-strewn pastures, snow-streaked ridgelines, and a silence that deepens with altitude. In early summer, the slopes below the refuge are flushed with gentians and alpine saxifrage; by late season, colors drain to ochre and gray, and the peaks rise bare and unadorned.

Refuge de Presset is more than a scenic overnight—it's a keystone in the mountaineering landscape of the Beaufortain. Most notably, it provides the primary base for ascents of the Pierra Menta, the iconic granite pillar that dominates the skyline and draws climbers

OPPOSITE: The hut can be accessed via the Col du Grand Fond, with its spectacular view of the Mont Blanc massif.
ABOVE: The modern interior has plenty of individual character.

and ski-mountaineers from across Europe. In summer, the hut sees alpinists preparing their racks for the classic southeast ridge, while in winter and spring, it becomes a crucible for the famed Pierra Menta ski mountaineering race—an epic four-day competition that tests the limits of endurance and camaraderie. To witness dawn break over the ridge, painting the needle of the Pierra Menta in pink and fire, is to understand why so many return to this place again and again.

There is history here, too, though not shouted. The original refuge was a modest shelter, built in the 1970s to serve the growing interest in ski touring. It was replaced in 2002 by the current structure, designed with sustainability in mind. Yet the soul of the place remains rooted in its role as a haven for skiers, climbers, and hikers alike.

At dusk, when the lake is still and the air thins to cold transparency, the silence feels ceremonial. In that hushed moment, the Refuge de Presset reveals its truest character—not as a monument, but as a threshold where ambition and awe meet, held gently in the comfort of the mountains.

OPPOSITE: The iconic Pierra Menta (2,714m) dominates the landscape and shares its name with the annual world-renowned ski-mountaineering race.

INDEX

CONTENTS

pp. 2–3

Photography by Aaron Rolph/
britishadventurecollective.com

INTRODUCTION

pp. 4–7

Photography by Aaron Rolph/
britishadventurecollective.com (pp. 5, 7);
Alessio Calo (pp. 4, 6)

BERGGASTHAUS AESCHER

pp. 190–197

Photography by Aaron Rolph/
britishadventurecollective.com

BIVAC II NA JEZERIH

pp. 130–137

Photography by Anže Čokl/anzecokl.com

BIVAC NA PREHODAVCIH

pp. 138–142

Photography by Anže Čokl/anzecokl.com

BIVACCO CHENTRE BIONAZ

pp. 42–45

Photography by Aaron Rolph/
britishadventurecollective.com

BIVACCO EDOARDO CAMARDELLA

pp. 46–51

Photography by Aaron Rolph/
britishadventurecollective.com

BIVACCO GERVASUTTI

pp. 26–33

Photography by Aaron Rolph/
britishadventurecollective.com (pp. 27–31, 33 top left);
Maurizio Marassi (p. 32);
Sami Sauri (p. 33 top right)

BIVACCO TITTA RONCONI

pp. 22–25

Photography by Aaron Rolph/
britishadventurecollective.com

BIVAK POD SKUTO

pp. 34–41

Photography by Aaron Rolph/
britishadventurecollective.com

BIVOUAC DES PÉRIADES

pp. 68–75

Photography by Aaron Rolph/
britishadventurecollective.com

BIVOUAC DU DOLENT

pp. 8–15

Photography by Aaron Rolph/
britishadventurecollective.com

CABANE DES VIGNETTES

pp. 52–57

Photography by Aaron Rolph/
britishadventurecollective.com

CABANE TORTIN

cabanetortin.com

pp. 120–129

Photography by Aube Media (pp. 121, 126 bottom);
G1 photos by Yves Garneau (pp. 122–125);
Albrecht Voss (pp. 126 top, 127–129)

CAPANNA REGINA MARGHERITA

pp. 220–229

Photography by Aaron Rolph/
britishadventurecollective.com

GAPPOHYTTA

pp. 152–157

Photography by Aaron Rolph/
britishadventurecollective.com

GRASSENBIWAK

pp. 114–119

Photography by Aaron Rolph/
britishadventurecollective.com

HANNIBAL BIVOUAC

pp. 198–205

Photography by Aaron Rolph/
britishadventurecollective.com

HOSPICE DU GRAND-SAINT-BERNARD
pp. 172–177

Photography by Aaron Rolph/
britishadventurecollective.com

JIM HABERL HUT
pp. 92–99

Photography by Mirae Campbell/
miraecampbell.com

JUBILÄUMSGRATHÜTTE
pp. 178–183

Photography by Aaron Rolph/
britishadventurecollective.com

KVERKFJÖLL MOUNTAIN HUT
pp. 100–105

Photography by Benjamin Hardman/
@benjaminhardman (pp. 101–103);
Eydís María Ólafsdóttir/
@eydismariaolafsdottir (pp. 104–105)

LALIDERERSPITZEN-BIWAK
pp. 206–213

Photography by Aaron Rolph/
britishadventurecollective.com

MONTE ROSA HÜTTE
pp. 214–219

Photography by Aaron Rolph/
britishadventurecollective.com

RABOTHYTTA
pp. 164–171

Photography by Linda Helland/
trailspotting.no (pp. 165–166, 169 top right),
Fabrice Milochau/@fab.milochau (pp. 167–168,
169 top left and bottom, 170–171)

RAMOLHAUS
pp. 230–237

Photography by Aaron Rolph/
britishadventurecollective.com

REFUGE DE L'AIGLE
pp. 184–189

Photography by Aaron Rolph/
britishadventurecollective.com

REFUGE DE PRESSET
pp. 246–253

Photography by Aaron Rolph/
britishadventurecollective.com (pp. 246–251);
Katie Hindson (p. 252); Louisa Treadwell (p. 253)

REFUGE DES BOUQUETINS
pp. 58–67

Photography by Aaron Rolph/
britishadventurecollective.com (pp. 59–61, 63–64);
Nathan Hughes (p. 62);
Mark James Chase (pp. 65, 66–67)

REFUGE DES GRANDS MULETS
pp. 144–151

Photography by Aaron Rolph/
britishadventurecollective.com (pp. 145–146, 148–149, 151);
Katie Hindson (pp. 147, 150)

RIFUGIO PASSO SANTNER
pp. 82–91

Photography by Fabian Dalpiaz Photography/
fabian-dalpiaz.com

SEFTON BIVOUAC
pp. 106–113

Photography by Sara Fondo/sarafondo.com (pp. 107–111);
Kavan Chay/kchayphotos.com (pp. 112–113)

SKÅPET
pp. 158–163

Photography by Tõnu Tunnel/tonutunnel.com

STÜDLHÜTTE
pp. 238–245

Photography by Max Draeger (pp. 239–241, 244–245);
Aaron Rolph/britishadventurecollective.com
(pp. 242–243)

SVARTTINDHYTTA
pp. 76–81

Photography by Aaron Rolph/
britishadventurecollective.com (pp. 77-78,80);
Maurizio Marassi (pp. 79, 81)

TEGERNSEER HÜTTE
pp. 16–21

Photography by Aaron Rolph/
britishadventurecollective.com

Alpine Refuges

The Architecture and Culture of Mountain Shelters

This book was edited and designed by gestalten.

Edited by Robert Klanten, Iris Hempelmann, and François-Luc Giraldeau
With Contributing Editor Aaron Rolph / britishadventurecollective.com

Text by Aaron Rolph

Photography (unless otherwise noted on pp. 254–255) by Aaron Rolph

Editorial management by Anna Diekmann

Design, layout, and cover design by Stefan Morgner

Cover image by Fabian Dalpiaz Photography / fabian-dalpiaz.com
Back cover image by Aaron Rolph / britishadventurecollective.com

Production management by Martin Bretschneider

Typefaces by Martin Majoor (Scala Sans)
and Jan Tschichold (Sabon)

Printed by Printer Trento S. p. a., Trento
Made in Europe

Published by gestalten, Berlin 2025
ISBN 978-3-96704-187-3
1st printing, 2025

© Die Gestalten Verlag GmbH & Co. KG, Berlin 2025

All rights reserved. No part of this publication may be reproduced or transmitted in any form or by any means, electronic or mechanical, including photocopying or any storage and retrieval system, without permission in writing from the publisher.

No part of this book may be used or reproduced in any manner for the purpose of training artificial intelligence technologies or systems. This work is reserved from text and data mining (Article 4 (3) Directive (EU) 2019/790).

Respect copyrights, encourage creativity!

For more information and to order books, please visit www.gestalten.com

Die Gestalten Verlag GmbH & Co. KG
Mariannenstrasse 9–10
10999 Berlin, Germany
hello@gestalten.com

Bibliographic information published by the Deutsche Nationalbibliothek
The Deutsche Nationalbibliothek lists this publication in the Deutsche Nationalbibliografie; detailed bibliographic data is available online at www.dnb.de

None of the content in this book was published in exchange for payment by commercial parties or designers; gestalten selected all included work solely on the basis of its artistic merit.

This book was printed on paper certified according to the standards of the FSC®.